A Voyage Round The World: In The Years 1800, 1801, 1802, 1803, And 1804, In Which The Author Visited The Principal Islands In The Pacific Ocean And The English Settlements Of Port Jackson And Norfolk Island, Volume 2

John Turnbull

SHIPWRECK
SEE PAGE 186

Turnbull

KBG

A

VOYAGE

ROUND

THE WORLD,

IN THE YEARS

1800, 1801, 1802, 1803, AND 1804;

IN WHICH

the Author visited the principal Islands

IN THE

PACIFIC OCEAN,

AND THE ENGLISH SETTLEMENTS OF

PORT JACKSON AND NORFOLK ISLAND.

BY JOHN TURNBULL.

IN THREE VOLUMES.

VOL. II.

London:

PRINTED FOR RICHARD PHILLIPS, No. 6, BRIDGE-
STREET, BLACKFRIARS.

By T. Gillet, Salisbury-square.

1805.

CONTENTS.

VOL. II.

———

CHAP. XVIII.

CHAP. XIX.

CHAP. XX.

CHAP. XXI.

CHAP. XXII.

CHAP. XXIII.

VOYAGES

IN THE

PACIFIC OCEAN.

—◆—

CHAP. XII.

Leave Ulitea.——Pass Bollabolla without having any Communication with the Natives.——Intercourse with the Natives of Maura.

THE hazards we had just experienced at Ulitea were so fresh in our minds, that although we passed near the island of Bollabolla, we made no attempt to open any intercourse with the inhabitants, who have the character of being daring pirates. They are said to have been originally such men as for their crimes had either fled or been banished from the surrounding islands. They are considered to be numerous, and the bravest warriors in all the Society Islands, and are a great terror to the Uliteans. The island of Bollabolla is distant from Uli-tea about six leagues, and may be easily distinguished from the other islands, by a very lofty double-peaked mountain, which may in good weather at sea be observed at the distance of fifteen leagues. The eastern side, as we sailed along it, had a very sterile appearance, and the island has not the same repute of fertility as Otaheite or Ulitea. As we made no stay, we can say nothing from our own experience, but that the distinguishing characteristic of these islanders, according to the report of their neighbours, is a more savage ferocity;

a circumstance consistent with their re-
puted original, that of having been fugitive criminals.

Our next station was the island called
Marra or Mobidie, being the most leeward
and smallest of the Society Islands.
It is only about fourteen or fifteen miles
in circuit, and appears to be surrounded
by a reef of coral rocks, which render
the approach to the shore very difficult.
We were told, however, by the natives,
that the lee side furnishes a good harbour for shipping; a circumstance, if
true, not known to our navigators, as
in every account of their southern voyages it is stated that this island has no
harbour. It is surrounded, in the same
manner as the neighbouring islands, by
one of those perilous coral reefs, which
render even the harbours of the Society Islands a very insufficient security,
and altogether none at all when the

wind blows with any violent degree of
strength from the sea. The east side of
the island produces cocoa-trees in great
abundance, and the bread-fruit here was
much larger, and of a better quality,
than any we had seen in the other islands
to windward : hogs, moreover, some
of which we procured, were much
cheaper than in the other islands. The
inhabitants appeared to us to differ in
no material respect from their neighbours in the other islands; and from
what was related to us on our return to
Port Jackson, their disposition seemed
to be of the same kind. When his majesty's ship the Porpoise was at this
island, the natives formed a scheme to
cut off her boat, in which were the
master, the surgeon, four seamen, and
two marines, all armed. The plot was,
however, happily discovered in time to
prevent the attempt, by the surgeon,

who was acquainted with the language
of the island. The object of the natives,
had their design succeeded, was to get
possession of the fire-arms in the boat;
and such is the eagerness with which
they covet those instruments of destruction, that there is no hazard they will
not run, no crime they will not perpe-
trate, to obtain possession of them. It
must be confessed, indeed, that local
circumstances give these articles a value the temptation of which cannot be
resisted by a common portion of honesty: a dozen of muskets might enable
them to repel, nay, perhaps subdue, their
neighbours, and if their ambition thus
overleaps all common restraints, it must
be lamented that there are others of a
more refined nation, who are not a
whit behind them in this weakness.

In this small island we found a chief
of Otaheite, who, for some misconduct,

had been obliged to exile himself, and had taken refuge here. This man's case served to confirm me in an opinion previously formed from observation, that the natives of Otaheite did not differ from those of the neighbouring islands so much in their personal character and dispositions, as in the nature of their government: and that the greater part of that seeming gentleness of manners for which they have been remarked, must be imputed rather to the power and authority of their king or principal chief than to their natural habits: this at least was certainly the case under the administration of our friend Pomarrie. And here again we had further proofs of the preference constantly given by the natives to articles of use, above others of mere ornament: beads, trinkets, looking-glasses, &c. were held in no estimation comparatively with knives, hatchets, muskets, or other instruments, to the utility of which they were no strangers. During our short stay among these islands, we had an opportunity of seeing two men who presented a most loathsome appearance. They were lepers, and seemed to have entirely lost their original skin, having the appearance of having been completely scalded from head to foot. These wretched beings, so much the object of abhorrence as well as of compassion in our eyes, were highly respected by their fellow islanders, as they were priests, and both of them considered men of no common sanctity in their eyes.

It is indeed one of the most singular traits amongst these savage nations, that their religion is not only tinctured, but apparently altogether composed of such ideas, as the nature of man most powerfully abhors. Their idea of a God, for a God, that is to say, a power above nature, they all acknowledge, is not that of a being beneficent, a common parent of nature, and a creator and benefactor of man : such is not the God of the Society Islands. On the contrary, the being they worship, is the being they fear, the being to whom they impute the destruction of their canoes, and the danger, the diseases, and deaths of their chiefs. Their diseases, and particularly those of their priests, are sacred, as the immediate effects of their power. These two lepers could not have been more revered, had they been prophets.

From this general character, that their deity is the offspring of their fears, may be induced the whole system of their mythology, and the attributes of their divinities. Hence it is, the idea of horror being connected with that of deformity, that representations of these Gods are usually either wholly shapeless or frightful.

CHAP. XIII.

Adieu to the Society Islands.—Ludicrous Circumstance in the Passage, between the Otaheitan Natives and our Seamen.— Arrival at the Sandwich Islands.—Commerce.—Trading.—Desertion of our Carpenter.

LEAVING Maura, we bid adieu for the present to the Society Islands, and stood on our course for the Sandwich Islands. This voyage furnished no occurrences out of the common order. The seamen, in their manner, amused themselves by representing to the natives of Otaheite on board the dangers that awaited them in crossing a certain part of the sea, meaning the equinoctial line, where they would certainly be harassed by infernal spirits rising out of the water. These stories had a powerful effect on the poor strangers, who had moreover for some time been extremely uneasy and impatient to see land once more, and appeared most sincerely to regret their imprudence in embarking on a voyage to which they could discover no bounds. So great was their terror at the moment, that I am persuaded had any land been in sight, they would have taken themselves off without leave; but as there was no back-door, they were compelled to submit to their fate; and their terror furnished an inexhaustible fund of amusement to our mischievous sailors.

In their distress they at last applied to be informed as to the truth of what the sailors had said, and on being unde-

ceived, gave a scope to their joy in the
most extravagant manner, leaping and
hallooing about the deck, as if their
minds had at once been relieved from
the most dreadful apprehensions. It was
however out of my power to prevent
them from going through the operation
of shaving, &c. usually performed by
seamen on persons crossing the line for
the first time, and considered by them
as too serious a privilege to surrender
to any remonstrance. We could discover that the whole of this business
had made a deep impression on the
Otaheitans, and that they promised
themselves much pleasure in recounting
their adventures to their countrymen
on their return; when the truth would
doubtless receive abundant embellish-
ment, for these islanders are naturally
fond of the marvellous, and are not
even scrupulous in the accounts they

give of any extraordinary events that fall in their way. The wind being scanty in the latter part of our voyage, the first land we made was Whahoo, an island subject to Tamahama, the great chief of the Sandwich Islands. Here we opened a trade with the inhabitants for salt, which we found much scarcer and dearer than we had expected. The increased price was occasioned, not only by the scarcity, but by the frequent intercourse the natives have with Europeans and Americans, from whom they have learned to affix a proper value to the productions of their country, and their bargains discover a knowledge and an acuteness very uncommon.

The Americans carry on in particular a most active trade with these islands, supplying them with property at an easy rate in exchange for provisions, and, unless I am much deceived, will do more than any others to exalt it to a singular degree of civilization. The reader will here pardon me for introducing this remark on American commerce: so far does it exceed all former efforts of former nations, that even the Dutch themselves sink under the comparison. Scarcely is there a part of the world, scarcely an inlet in these most unknown seas, in which this commercial hive has not penetrated. The East-Indies is open to them, and their flags are displayed in the seas of China. And it must be confessed, to their honour, that their success is well merited by their industry.

In order to accommodate the natives in bringing off their articles for sale, or rather barter, we kept the ship as close as possible in with the land: but then we were beset with such numbers of men and women, that our vessel could not have contained a quarter of our visitors, had we been disposed to admit them on board. To prevent this embarrassment, we resolved as much as possible to assume the appearance of a ship of war; and therefore dressed six seamen in soldiers' uniforms, and made them walk the deck under arms, and kept our colours and pendant always flying. These precautions we had reason to believe were not unnecessary, for it was in this island that the captain and the astronomer of his majesty's ship Dædalus lost their lives in an affray with the natives. The exemplary manner in which their murder was revenged by captain Vancouvre, has been very beneficial to all navigators who since his time have touched at the island. A few similar instances of justice would have more efficacy in ensuring the safety of our intercourse with this people, than any of those wanton and ill-judged cruelties which, under the circumstance of the slightest quarrel with these natives, are but too commonly practised.

The natives showed the utmost eagerness to get on board the ship; but when all their attempts were opposed, and themselves forced back into their canoes by our new-made marines, they at last contented themselves with lying at a little distance, conversing with our Otaheitan natives. After some time, appeared one of the deputy chiefs of the island, under Tamahama, whose approach created no small stir and bustle among the other islanders in their endeavouring to open a passage for him. But as many of their canoes were crowded and entangled together, they were in the hurry run down by the canoe of this great man, who took not the least notice of the disasters he had so wantonly occasioned, or rather who affected this cavalier behaviour, with the intention of impressing us with a high idea of his rank and consequence in the country. The poor natives, recovering their canoes, cleared them of the water, got into them again, and remained near the ship, without expressing the smallest dissatisfaction or complaint on account of the tyrannical treatment of the chief. When he was received on board, he immediately commenced inspector-general of all commodities brought off to us for sale; and at last, whether justly or unjustly I know not, he seized an old man whom he charged with offering for sale some salt belonging to the king. The old man was so alarmed at this charge, that he seemed ready to expire with terror; so that we interposed in his behalf, and on our account he was pardoned, and set at liberty. Whilst he was on board, he released us from the embarassment of our numerous visitors : seem, ingly resolved that we should be troubled with no other impertinence but his own. He commanded the canoes to remove to a greater distance, and issued his mandates in a tone of authority which would not have disgraced a bashaw. He appeared to entertain an equal indifference to any mischief he might cause; for as many of his countrymen as were in any degree tardy in obeying his mandate, he saluted with stones from our ballast, which maimed not a few of them.

Nor did the natives appear to oppose any resistance, but submitted, as if to an acknowledged authority, without murmur or reluctance. In these islands, indeed, obedience is understood as well as tyranny, and the despotism and wantonness of command in the chiefs is only equalled by the correspondent timidity and submission of the people. Philosophers are much mistaken who build systems of natural liberty. Rousseau's savage, a being who roves the woods according to his own will, exists no where but in his writings.

Although we could not but abhor the despotic conduct of this chief, yet to it we were indebted for the clearing of the ship from crowds of natives, who were endeavouring on all hands to come on board. He had however with him some friends, whom he requested leave to introduce to us, and to whom on his account we shewed what civilities appeared to be proper.

We remained only a few days in this island, salt being so scarce that we were obliged to remove the ship to several different places to glean what could be found. When our business was over, we settled our accounts with the chief just mentioned, who was receiver-general for the king. He then left the ship, and, to our astonishment, was accompanied by every native, taking to their paddles, and making for the land with all possible speed. One canoe, the one which had brought off one of Tamahama's naval officers, alone remained. We enquired of this person the meaning of the sudden departure of his country-men, but he declared he was totally ig-norant of the cause, and neither could nor would give us any satisfaction. Being apprehensive of some treacherous pro-jects against us, either on the part of the islanders or of their chiefs, it at first oc-curred to us to secure the person of this officer as a pledge for our safety; but on further consideration of the difficul-ties to which this step might expose not only us, but other future European na-vigators, we judged it most prudent to suffer him to depart.

As soon as he had left us, beginning now to suspect the true cause of the hasty departure of our visitors, I made enquiry amongst our people whether they had not found means to steal some articles belonging to the ship; and from their general precipitation, and general flight, my mind suggested to me that the theft was of no ordinary consequence. It was some time before I could procure a satisfactory answer; but it was at length discovered that our carpenter had secretly conveyed himself into one of the canoes, and had thus been carried on shore.

Such is the difficulty, nay almost impossibility, of maintaining the necessary complement of men in these voyages, that I could almost recommend that no one should hazard the attempt, unless, as in a king's ship, he can support his authority by martial law. Nothing, as we have before mentioned, can withstand the seduction and artifices of the southern islanders; women, and a life of indolence, are too powerful for the sense of duty in the minds of our seamen. Had we relaxed our efforts for a single moment, our ship would have been deserted.

The acquisition of such a person was of inestimable value to Tamahama, and there seemed to be little doubt that, conscious of the value of their prize, they would defend it with their utmost efforts. Our force, moreover, was wholly inadequate to compel them to restore him; and in endeavouring to recover one of our ship's company, we should have run the risk of losing many more by similar desertion. From these and other reasons, we thought it more prudent to put up with our loss; although of a person whom we could so ill spare.

CHAP. XIII.

*Departure from Whahoo.—Arrival at At-
towaie.—Visited by the King, and General of the Island.—Tamahama's Determination to invade them.—Friendly Reception.*

ALTHOUGH the island of Whahoo is
one of the most fruitful in the dominions of Tamahama, and that the natives
supplied us with an abundance of all necessary articles, yet the demands of the
sellers were much higher than we had
either reason to expect, or could indeed
afford. The natives have indeed profited sufficiently by their intercourse with
navigators, to know the greater value of
their country produce than at what
they had hitherto rated it.

One of these islanders had the modesty to demand the ship's main-sail in
barter for four hogs. In all their bargains they would have their choice of
whatever articles they wished in exchange, and as much of these as they
wanted; no business could otherwise be
done, and they returned with their
wares to the shore. We were therefore
obliged to confine our dealings to what
was indispensably requisite for the use
of the ship and crew.

Here we were informed that the king
Tamahama, attended by the greater
part of his chiefs, was at present at
Mouie. It is the wise policy of this chief,
that all those who possess any authority
or influence in the country, should accompany him in his progress through
his dominions, that he may have them
constantly under his eye, and not leave
them exposed to the seductions and con-
spiracies of his rival chiefs. These are

continually in pursuit of the means of throwing off his yoke, and rendering themselves independent as well of him, and of each other, as of their former king.

For this precaution, moreover, he assigns his own experience, that once being absent on an expedition to a neighbouring island, an insurrection was fomented in his absence, and that it was not without much difficulty that he could restore his authority. Since that time he has never given the chiefs the same opportunity; it is the chiefs alone he dreads, for he observes that there is no danger to be apprehended from the lower order whilst separated from the chiefs. From further information received here, Tamahama seems to be making rapid progress in his schemes of aggrandisement. After having defeated the rightful sovereign of this island of

Whahoo, and all the kings of the islands to the eastward, he has forced him, after many ineffectual struggles, to take refuge in the island of Attowaie. Thus the sovereign authority over all those islands remains in his family, and his power and riches, from his intercourse with shipping, was hourly increasing. He was at this time making great preparations to exterminate the fugitive king even from his place of refuge. So intent was he on this invasion, that the chief anxiously demanded of us our next destination, and whether we intended touching at Attowaie. He was urgent to obtain a passage for himself and another, to act as spies. We excused ourselves in the best possible way, observing it much depended upon circumstances, and thus cleared ourselves of the importunities of these emissaries of this Alexander of the Sandwich Islands.

Leaving Whahoo, we directed our course to another island to the leeward, called Attowaie; but the wind was so unfavourable, that we could not weather the south part of this island; we therefore stood along close under the north shore, proceeding slowly to give the natives an opportunity of guessing the object of our visit. It was not long before some of the islanders came off to us; they requested us to anchor until they should return, and inform their countrymen of our arrival upon their coasts.

Amongst these islanders the arrival of an European vessel is an event of the first political importance; an event in which king and people are equally concerned. The Otaheitans receive us with the satisfaction of friends; the Sandwich islanders have reached more than one gradation higher in the scale of ci-

vilization, and, understanding their own
interest, consider their European visitors as the importers of new arts, and
new skill and industry, into their country. The voyage of Vancouvre has
made a most eminent and permanent
change in the situation of the Sandwich
islanders. They have taken a leap as it
were into civilization, and, if their progress keep any pace with the vigour of
their first start, they will not be long
considered as savages.

In the interval of waiting the arrival
of our promised visitors, we fitted up
our temporary marines, and made every
other preparation that might make a favourable impression on the minds of the
natives.

As soon as it was made known on
shore that a ship had appeared off the
coast, with an intention to stop and take
in supplies, the commander in chief or

generalissimo was dispatched to welcome us in the name of the king.

This personage appeared in a most beautiful canoe; he seemed to be over-joyed at our arrival, and apologised on account of the lateness of the hour, for his master's not waiting on us in person.

He was particularly inquisitive respect-ing the situation of affairs at Whahoo, and the state of the preparations made by Tamahama for the threatened inva-sion of the island. We explained to him that however painful it was to us to be messengers of disagreeable tidings, we could give him no encouragement to hope that Tamahama had laid aside his project; for that every thing seemed to show his determination to attempt it as speedily as the necessary preparations would allow. This the chief said he al-ready had learned, and was now grieved to have the news confirmed by strangers, who had no possible interest in deluding him.

It was easy to see how much this information affected him, for, from being extremely gay and communicative, as when he first came on board, he instantly became melancholy and taciturn. He was a near relation of the king, and had steadily adhered to him in all his misfortunes. They were now cooped up with a small body of faithful followers, but were firmly resolved to oppose to the utmost the attacks of Tamahama.

May the efforts of their courage and patriotism give an awful lesson to their ambitious conqueror, that courage in a good cause, animated by despair, is a sufficient overbalance for even a greater inequality of force! Tamahama is no unworthy imitator of his European original. His haughty tone to his enemies, and his genius and spirit of enterprise

in creating resources which did not exist before him, may not unjustly bring
him into a comparison with the empe-
ror of the French.

To change the gloomy current of our
visitor's thoughts, we exhibited before
him some articles of British manufacture; he commended them indeed, but
with the air of carelessness of one whose
mind was possessed with objects of a
more immediate interest. He inquired
frequently whether we had on board
any fire-arms or gun-powder, in the expectation that we would furnish them
with at least a small supply of each.
This, however, we thought proper to
decline, endeavouring to make him
comprehend that our stock was far from
being sufficient for ourselves, under
the numberless occasions we might have
of self-defence before we could either
return to our own country, or procure
farther supplies.

In the evening, when the captain was examining some charts of those seas, the chief looked earnestly over him, and begged that their island might be pointed out to him. This was done, and he expressed great pleasure in finding that even their little corner had not been omitted. When night came on, the chief requested that some covering might be provided for the natives who attended him. This was readily complied with, as we had an abundant stock of cloth of the manufacture of Otaheite. This was extremely well received; and presented to our Otaheitans an opportunity of pointing out, with no little satisfaction, all its good qualities, as well as of displaying to the strangers the vast wealth and power of their own sovereigns, Pomarrie and Otoo; the main point of their eloquence being to prove the prodigious superiority of Otaheite over all other quarters of the world. The long voyage they had accomplished in our ship was not forgotten; and on this they valued themselves highly, as giving them an infinite advantage over all other islanders.

The chief retired early to rest; but his attendants and their new friends from Otaheite, whose language, complexion, and manners, so nearly resembled their own, were too highly delighted with each other, to be prevailed on to part until after midnight.

The exiled king of these islands bears a character infinitely superior in a moral point of view at least, to that of his more powerful rival Tamahama. The fidelity of former dependants in a season of misfortune and fallen power, is surely no doubtful testimony of the virtues of a conquered king; and the virtue of this chief, if measured according to this standard, is great indeed. He appeared to be loved almost to adoration, and his authority from influence seemed to be increased almost in the same proportion as his actual power had become diminished. Is it not a phenomenon in the political world, that the greater part of all unhappy revolutions, revolts, and conquests, usually happen under such kings? It is not to the honour of the generosity of our nature, that we are thus inclined to avail ourselves of that confidence and lenity, which always characterises power in the hands of a benevolent nature?

On the following morning we received a visit from this good king, and were welcomed very heartily by him to Attowaie. His skin was covered with a greyish scurf, probably occasioned by the immoderate use of the *ava*. This loathsome disease had made a greater progress on the person of this man, than on that of any other we had before seen; although at Otaheite we had met with very severe cases of the same distemper. He laboured under a great depression of spirits, and could not refrain from complaining of certain reports propagated by some Englishmen settled under his enemy Tamahama, which had prevented several vessels from touching at his island for refreshments. He declared himself to be a fast friend of the English; and produced very favourable certificates of his conduct, from several captains with whom he had dealings.

From some Englishmen who had followed his fortunes for several years, this unfortunate chief had acquired such an acquaintance with our language, that he was able to understand and answer any plain question we put to him.

This appeared the more extraordinary, as even the natives of Otaheite, notwithstanding their greater opportunities, have hitherto made so little progress in our language, that even the proper names of those with whom they were best acquainted, are hardly to be known in their mouths. The king was as anxious as the other chief had been, to receive accounts of his enemy's motions; and equally distressed with the information we afforded, as being fully aware of the inevitable consequences of an attack by Tamahama. He brought off a present of yams, plantains, and a couple of hogs, assuring us that every thing in the island was at our disposal. He professed a high regard for the British nation; and as a proof of it, had taken to himself the name of *king George*, and to his children, who were numerous, he had given those of the present royal family of England, beginning with the *prince of Wales*, and descending to the youngest branch of the family.

In this distribution, however, some irregularities had taken place; as his information had been procured from the English residing with him, who were not over-accurate in their genealogical knowledge. His conversation repeatedly turned to his want of fire-arms and gunpowder; but we contrived to avoid making any engagements on this subject.

Observing the deep despondency into which the king's affairs had thrown him, our humanity averted from the idea of suffering him to have any spirits or intoxicating liquors; a present he doubtless expected, though he had the singular modesty to make no mention of it.

The dilemma in which I had been involved at Otaheite with Edeah and her gallant, made me ever afterwards very

cautious in this respect with the natives
of these islands. Their passions are naturally impetuous; and when fed by the
fuel of strong liquors, acknowledge no
restraint. I know no sufficient punishment that the wretch would merit who
should import a cargo of spirituous liquors into the Sandwich or Society
Islands; it would in every respect be
tantamount to the wilful administration
of an equal quantity of poison, as the
extent of the evil would only be boun-
ded by the destruction of the whole of
the population.

CHAP. XIV.

Strong attachment of the Natives to their present Sovereign.—Desperate Resolution of this man in case of Invasion.—Departure for Onehow.

THIS unhappy man, who, from every thing we saw and heard, is well deserving of a better fate, had already suffered so much from the ambition and power of Tamahama, that he was now about to adopt one of the most extravagant resolutions that can be conceived.

The Europeans who had attached themselves to his fortunes, some of whom were carpenters, blacksmiths, &c. were now with their offspring a numerous body. As their last resource, they were constructing a vessel suited to the attempt of a long voyage, and in the event of the expected invasion, they proposed to escape from the island, and seek a refuge from the cruelty of their enemy in some one of the islands which they have heard are interspersed in the main sea.   They are wholly ignorant of the method of measuring a ship's course, or of the other necessary branches of navigation.   A compass, indeed, they possess.   Their intention in the first place, is, to steer to the westward, in the hope of reaching some part of the coast of China ; or, by keeping their wind to the southward, to fall in with Otaheite, or, some other of the Society Islands.   Dreadful alternative! and in fact the case is desperate, for they are well aware that resistance is in vain when once invaded.   Perhaps, in the whole catalogue of human misery, there is not one more poignant, and more the object of pity to a generous mind, than that of a whole people becoming thus the victims of the ambition of one man, and, to satisfy his lust of conquest, expelled from their native home. The most pathetic pieces of poetry in any language, are the lamentations of the Spanish Moors upon t ir pulsion from Spain. The love of country is never understood, till we consider it as lost or endangered. I cannot speak of this unfortunate people without a melancholy involuntarily seizing on the train of my ideas.

Extravagant as this scheme of emigration may appear, in a people so destitute of the proper means for executing it, yet it is not improbable that by such enterprises in different periods of time, the most distant islands may have been peopled, and a similar language and mode of life established in quarters which seem to have no possible means of intercourse.

In Otaheite the same means have not unfrequently been proposed for escaping from the fury of a victorious foe; as in the case of old Pomarrie, who in his distresses has repeatedly applied to European navigators to convey him to some distant spot, where, removed from the attempts of his rivals, he might live free from danger.

Even our sailors were much affected by the unhappy situation of this chief, for he was by far the most intelligent native of these seas; and the ardent affection of his dependants and subjects was an ample testimony of his worth.

During our stay in the island, he never left the ship, but ordered whatever we wanted to be brought off to us, and was obeyed with the greatest cheerfulness and

punctuality.. As he had made such a progress in the English language, his conversation was at once entertaining and in-
structive to us; and had his mind been
more at ease, and his affairs in a more
prosperous situation, a very advantageous connection might have been established between us.

His presence on board encouraged the
islanders to bring off considerable supplies
of salt, so that in a short time we made
great progress in our business. When the
labours of the day were over, we entertained the king, with his relation the general, and the other attendants, with a
dance and song, performed by our Otaheitan natives, in which Pulpit's young
wife bore a principal share. As the women of the. Sandwich Islands are generally of a coarse masculine appearance,
and nut-brown complexion, this young
Otaheitan, who was a very good sample
of her countrywomen, passed for a

beauty in this place. The king was himself pleased to term her a very pretty
girl. On this occasion he took an opportunity of informing me that he
had sent an ambassador all the way to
Otaheite, to negociate with Otoo for a
wife; and observed that as we had come
from thence he expected that the man
would have embraced that opportunity
of returning in our ship with the object
of his mission. Indeed, previous to our
leaving Otaheite, this man had solicited a
passage home, having been unsuccessful
in his application to Otoo; we assented
to his wish, but the night previous to our
departure he swam on shore from the
ship, thus forgetting his duty and allegiance to his sovereign, through the
preponderating influence of Otoo, who
had seduced him from a falling cause.

The king's attendants were resolved
not to be outdone on this occasion; and

displayed their ingenuity in the same way, exerting themselves to the utmost for the entertainment of the company. At last our own tars, that they might contribute their proportion to the delights of the spectators, produced a violin; and one of them, who was an excellent dancer, performed a hornpipe in such perfection, that all the strangers joined in acknowledging that our music and our dancing were far superior to their own. We perceived with pleasure that these amusements seemed to afford a temporary relief to the unhappy king; he seemed for a moment to forget his cares, and participate in the satisfaction of his subjects. Would that we could have effectually dissipated his anxiety!

As soon as we arrived on the coast of this island, we found it necessary to employ every precaution to prevent any further desertion from the ship;

and being persuaded that we might count on the fidelity of Pulpit, whom we had taken on board at Ulitea, and who had already rejected all the offers of the king, who earnestly wished to retain him as an assistant, we admitted him into the cabin mess, whilst his Otaheitan lady ate with our cabin boy. This separation was not occasioned by her attachment to the customs of Otaheite, where the sexes always eat apart; but in fact the behaviour of this poor female being not always governed by what is considered as correct propriety in Europe, she was not altogether the most desirable companion at our table.

In the course of my stay at Attowaie, we had many opportunities to observe the dispositions and conduct of the king. One night, the wind increasing to a storm, we were driven out of sight of the island, and were two days in regaining our station. All this time the king expressed the greatest concern for his family and friends on shore, without seeming in any degree alarmed for himself. On returning to our former situation, it occurred to the king to make an experiment of the regard really entertained for him by the natives. When the first canoe came alongside, the king concealed himself in the cabin, directing one of his attendants to say that we had landed him on the island of Whahoo, and delivered him up as a prisoner to the authority of his grand enemy Tamahama. This canoe, belonging to the king himself, was loaded with provisions for his use; amongst which were some young dogs, esteemed in these islands a peculiar delicacy, and therefore kept for the tables of the great alone.

The dogs of the Society and Sand-

wich Islands are indeed very different
from the same animals in Europe.
They are very carefully fed, and any
thing that might render their flesh
coarse and strong, kept out of their
way; by this means they were said rather to resemble kid than dogs, and are
not unfrequently tasted by our hungry
sailors.

Not seeing their master upon the
deck, the islanders enquired earnestly
how and where he was: being told
he was now a prisoner in Whahoo,
they laughed heartily at the supposed
jest; but as all their countrymen on
board agreed in a serious repetition of
this assertion, they were struck dumb
with astonishment and grief. Never
was affection, never was the terror of
genuine loyalty, more strongly impress-
ed, than on the countenances of these
honest subjects of an unfortunate king.

It was gratifying to a generous mind to witness this affectionate testimony, as well of the fidelity of the subjects, as of the worth of the chief. This was no flattery; it was the generous, the honourable impulse of an honest nature.

After sometime, they recovered themselves so far as to renew their enquiries, with looks aghast with terror. They eagerly demanded how this disaster had happened; at the same time condemning themselves for suffering him to remain on board the ship, and be exposed to such a misfortune. When their despair was wrought to the highest pitch, the poor king, who witnessed the whole scene, could no longer contain his feeling; but running upon deck, showed himself to the natives, reproaching them kindly for so readily believing that we could have so betrayed him into the hands of enemies. The sudden tran-

sition from grief to joy produced the
most lively and affecting change on these
faithful creatures. We could not however so far recover them from their ter-
rors, as not to intreat the king to leave
the ship, that he might not be again
driven from the island, and exposed to
some serious accident. To this he good-
naturedly agreed; and was preparing to
leave our vessel, when a large double canoe came alongside with an European
on board.

His errand was to acquaint the king,
that a report having reached the island
of his having fallen into the hands of
Tamahama, the inhabitants were become disorderly, and that nothing but
his appearance amongst them could restore tranquillity. The good king now
appeared, and it must be confessed with
good reason, much happier than before;
he seemed to collect new hope from this

testimony of the love of his people, and to forget all his danger in the pleasing reflection that he was thus beloved. I am persuaded that, animated with this love for their chief, had the numbers of this good people been even in a small degree more proportionable to that of their enemy, even the warlike Tama-hama would not have found them an easy conquest. But their strength is too unequal to indulge any expectation of even safety in resistance. They have indeed but one resource left, that of flight in their new-built ship; and desperate, and apparently chimerical, as this is, it promises more success than the chance of war.

His immediate departure being now indispensable, I enquired what we could do to express our sense of his many favours? To this he answered, that if we really were his good friends, we would supply him with whatever we could conveniently spare of iron, canvas, and other necessaries for his new vessel.

Having a good stock of iron, I furnished him with as much as he thought sufficient for his purpose, together with some tools, axes &c.; crowning our presents with a few looking-glasses, a quantity of English cloth, and a small supply of gunpowder.

These articles this good man accepted with the most affecting demonstration of genuine heartfelt gratitude; and entering his canoe, he requested us on our return home to mention his hard fate to our countrymen; he concluded with pouring out benedictions upon us, and at length, having finished his adieus, he rowed for the shore with the greatest dispatch.

The melancholy fate of this chief, his strange reverse of fortune, and the dismal prospects still awaiting him, joined to the goodness of his conduct and character, had completely enlisted us on his side; and we could not but earnestly hope, that he might in the event triumph over his grand enemy Tamahama.

We almost regretted that captain Vancovre had ever touched at the island of Tamahama; as from his assistance principally had this chief obtained that addition to his former strength, which, improved by his uncommon talents, had enabled him to become a conqueror and usurper. Had captain Vancouvre foreseen the consequence of his encouragement of this ambitious chief, I am persuaded he would have received the advances of Tamahama in a very different manner; but we are all blind instruments in the hands of an overruling Providence, and it is some consolation that all this is not without some purpose of good, though it may exceed our powers to comprehend it.

We had now procured a good stock of salt, but not sufficient to answer our purpose; and having come so far, we were very unwilling to return without the completion of our plan. We had now no resource left, but to return to one or other of the islands under the command of Tamahama. We were already aware of the difficulty of procuring ship provisions in the islands belonging to this chief, not only on account of the high price required by the natives, but that no articles would be received in exchange but precisely such as the sellers should choose. To obviate as much as was practicable these difficulties, we bore up for Onehow, the other small island still remaining faithful to the rightful king of Atowaie; who, previously knowing our in-

tention offered to accompany us in person; but it appearing more prudent that
he should remain for the present where
he was, he dispatched a messenger before us to Onehow, informing the natives of our intended visit, and directing them to treat us with every attention, and supply our wants.

This notice produced its full effect; for
on our making the island, the natives
flocked off to us, furnishing abundance
of yams at a very moderate value; we
there also laid in a small addition to
our stock of salt. Here, as at the other
islands, all were eager to be admitted on
board; but the notion of our ship being
a man of war, and the formidable appearance of our marines, kept them in
awe. We received none in the ship but
one of the king's deputies, and, through
the interest of this great man, two
other chiefs. We found, from the lan-

guage of these persons, as also of the other natives, that they were stedfastly attached to their lawful king, and determined so to remain, although they had but little hope of being able to withstand the attacks of their common enemy Tamahama.

CHAP. XV.

Leave the Leeward Islands, and proceed to Windward.—Arrival at Owhyhee. —Commence Trading.—Visited by Mr. Young.

HAVING in the course of four days collected about three tons of yams, an invaluable treasure to us in such circumstances, we set sail to the eastward for Owhyhee, and there renewed our intercourse with the natives, who, as has been already mentioned, were complete masters of their business. Every article we wanted was at least three times, many of them six times, the price they would have borne at the island we had just left.

Soon after our arrival we received a visit from our countryman, Mr. Young, who had resided there for fourteen years past; from whom we had a confirmation of the particulars respecting Tamahama communicated to us at Whahoo, and of his erecting a royal residence at Mouie, and, above all, of his fixed determination to attempt the conquest of the two other islands, of Attowaie and Onehow.

His palace is built after the European style, of brick, and glazed windows, having European and American artificers about him of almost every description. Indeed his own subjects, from their intercourse with Europeans, have acquired a great knowledge of several of the mechanical arts, and have thus enabled him to increase his navy, a very favourite object with him. I have no doubt that in a very few years he will erect amongst these

islands a power very far from despi-
cable.

The circumstances of this enterprising chief were greatly changed since the
visit of captain Vancouvre, to whom,
as to the servant and representative of
the king of Great Britain, with much
formality and ceremony, he had made a
conveyance of the sovereignty of Owhyhee, in the hopes of being thus more
strongly confirmed in his authority, and
supplied with the means of resisting his
enemies.

His dominion seems now to be completely established. He is not only a
great warrior and politician, but a very
acute trader, and a match for any European in driving a bargain. He is well
acquainted with the different weights
and measures, and the value which all
articles ought to bear in exchange with
each other; and is ever ready to take

the advantage of the necessities of those who apply to him or his people for supplies.

His subjects have already made considerable progress in civilization; but are held in the most abject submission, as Tamahama is inflexible in punishing all offences which seem to counteract his supreme command.

It was only in 1792 that captain Vancouvre laid down the keel of Tamahama's first vessel, or rather craft; but so assiduously has he applied himself to effect his grand and favourite object, the establishment of a naval force, that at the period of our arrival he had upwards of twenty vessels of different sizes, from twenty-five to fifty tons; some of them were even copper-bottomed.

He was, however, at this time much in want of naval stores; and, to have his navy quickly placed on a respectable footing, would pay well for them. He has also a certain number of body-guards to attend him, independently of the number of chiefs who are required to accompany him on all his journies and expeditions.

In viewing this man, my imagination suggested to me that I beheld in its first progress one of those extraordi-nary natures which, under other circum-stances of fortune and situation, would have ripened into the future hero, and caused the world to resound with his feats of glory. What other was Philip of Macedon, as pictured by the Gre-cian historians? a man who over-came every disadvantage of slight re-sources and powerful rivals, and ex-tended the narrow sovereignty of Ma-cedon into a universal monarchy of Greece, and the known world.

Some convicts from Botany Bay, hav-

ing effected their escape to the Sandwich
Islands, rendered themselves at first ser-
vicable to Tamahama, and, in recompence, were put in possession of small
portions of land for cultivation. On
these they raised some sugar-canes, and
at last contrived to distil a sort of spirit,
with which they entertained each other
by turns, keeping birth-days and other
holidays; until Tamahama, finding that
such festivities greatly retarded his work,
made some gentle representations on the
subject.

This lenity, however, producing no
good effect, but the drinking, idleness,
and quarrels among the new settlers,
seeming rather to become more frequent than before, and their insolence
being carried so far as to insult and mal-
treat many of the natives, Tamahama
gave the strangers to understand, that
in their next fighting-party he would
make one of the company, and see who

could best acquit himself on the occasion. This hint produced the desired effect: the Botany Bay settlers were soon brought into complete submission, and a due sense of their situation.

These particulars were collected from Mr. Young; a man of strict veracity, who, having been long in the country, had the best opportunities to know the truth. He has been long in the confidence of Tamahama, whose fortunes he has constantly followed from the beginning, and who gives him daily proofs of the sincerity of his attachment. He added, that for several years Tamahama had adopted it as a rule, to request from all Europeans who touched within his dominions, a certificate or testimonial of his good conduct towards them; but that now considering his character for honesty and civility to be established, he no longer deems such certificates of any important use.

Tamahama's ardent desire to obtain a ship from captain Vancouvre, was in all probability first excited by the suggestions of Young and his countryman Davis: but such was the effect of this undertaking, that Tamahama became immediately more sparing of his visits on board the Discovery; his time being now chiefly employed in attending to the carpenters at work on this new man of war, which, when finished, was named the Britannia. This was the beginning of Tamahama's navy; and from his own observations, with the assistance of Messrs. Young, Davis, &c., he has laboured inflexibly in improving his marine force, until he has brought it to its present perfection; securing to him not only a decided superiority over the frail canoes of his neighbours, but the means of transporting his warriorrs to distant parts. Some of his vessels are employed as transports in carrying provisions from one island to another to supply his warriors ; whilst the largest are used as men of war, and are occasionally mounted with a few light guns. No one better understands his interest than this ambitious chief: no one better knows how to improve an original idea. The favours of Vancouvre, and his other European benefactors, would have been thrown away on any other savage ; but Tamahama possesses a genius above his situation.

His body-guards, who may be considered in some respects as regularly disciplined troops, go on duty and relieve each other as in Europe, calling out *all is well* at every half-hour, as on board ship. Their uniform at this time was simply a blue great-coat with yellow facings.

With other things which Tamahama has learned by intercourse with Europeans, he has acquired a relish for our spirits, so that some navigators have exchanged their rum with him to very good account; sometimes when his stock of liquor is exhausted, he employs the Europeans settled in his dominions to extract spirits from the sugar canes, which grow there of an excellent quality. When Tamahama means to relax from his serious occupations, he invites his own wives and those of his chiefs to share his regale of spirits, which in its operation seldom fails to create disputes and even quarrels among the ladies, to the great entertainment of the master of the feast and the other male guests.

The natives of the Sandwich Islands are in every respect much more ingenious, and much further advanced in the knowledge of the useful arts of life, than those of Otaheite. It is true that the former are excelled by the latter in the manufacture of cloth; but the spears, the clubs, mats, calibashes, fish-hooks, and other implements of the Sandwich Islanders, are far superior to similar articles made in Otaheite, whose inhabitants are not much regarded by their northern neighbours. The natives of Bollabola, on the contrary, are esteemed by the natives of the Sandwich Islands as the bravest and most expert warriors of the Society Islands; every thing being good, according to their adage, that comes from Bollabola. A number of the Sandwich Islanders have at different periods passed to Otaheite, where they find every encouragement to settle from the young king Otoo, who, from their superior skill and warlike disposition, generally prefers them as the attendants on his person.

During our stay at Atowaie, one of these Sandwich Islands, we observed the king and his fighting general made use

of spitting boxes inlaid with the teeth
of their enemies slain in battle; and this
practice, joined to other circumstances,
observed at the time of their being discovered by captain Cook, leads to the
belief that human beings were not unfrequently their food. Indeed they were
confessedly canibals at the time of their
discovery.

The Sandwich Islands are extremely
well peopled, all circumstances of their
nature and fertility being considered:
and the women, according to Mr.
Young's account, are said to be more
numerous than the men; whereas in
Otaheite the women are not reckoned
to amount to more than one tenth part
of the population.

The striking difference in the population of these two spots may in a great
measure be imputed to the absence from
Owhyhee of the horrid practice of in-

fant murder. This increased population
of the Sandwich Islands has had one
good effect; it has compelled the natives
to exert themselves in assisting nature by
the more careful cultivation of the soil,
and other branches of industry. The
tarra, yam, and sweet potatoe, are
productions common to all the islands;
but are found in the greatest plenty in
those which lie to leeward, and are
cheapest in Atowaie and Onehow,
from whence we took on board three
tons of yams, and twenty hogs; articles which would have cost a considerable sum in any of the islands subject to
Tamahama. These islands also produce most of the tropical fruits; me-
lons, shaddocks, pompions, plantains,
and bananas, are here in great abundance. They likewise furnish Indian
corn, but not in a great quantity. The
sugar-canes are here of excellent quality.

'The mountain plantain is of the greatest service to the natives; for with these, some cocoa-nut water, and a little *mahie* (a sour paste made of the bread-fruit when ripe), well beat up together, they make a dish called *pop poye*, eaten by all ranks from the king to the lowest of the inhabitants. The same food is universally used in Otaheite.

CHAP. XVI.

*Enterprising Spirit of the Sandwich Island-
ers.—Knowledge of our Language.—
Dexterity in diving.—Desertion of the
Otaheitan Natives.—Tamahama's Intention of opening a Trade with China.*

THE Sandwich Islanders in the dominions of Tamahama, frequently make voyages to the north-west coast of America.
and thereby acquire sufficient property to
make themselves easy and comfortable, as
well as respectable among their countrymen; to whom, on their return home,
they are fond of describing with great
emphasis and extravagance the singular
events of their voyage. Several of them

have made considerable progress in the
English language; their intercourse
with the Anglo-Americans, and the navigators from Britain, having given
them the opportunity, of which they
have so eagerly availed themselves.

The canoes of the Sandwich Islands
far surpassed any that we had seen in
other parts of the world; not only in
solidity and strength, but in the neat-
ness and skill of workmanship. These
canoes are so well calculated for speed,
that we have seen the natives work
them along with their short paddles at
the rate of eleven or twelve miles in an
hour, and fairly run them under water.

Although they have these excellent
canoes in abundance, the natives, both
men and women, often dispense with
the use of them, and swim to vessels
approaching the island, with no other
support than a thin feather-edged slice of

wood: with these they play a thousand tricks, tumbling and plunging one another into the water, then rising to the surface and plunging again, like so many inhabitants of the deep.

Their fondness for the water is indeed singular. They may be sometimes seen extended and lolling indolently on the water for the whole day, without any occupation, and as much at their ease as if it was their native element. Instances are very rare, I believe, of the Sandwich Islanders being drowned; their boldness and dexterity in diving is perhaps unrivalled in any part of the world. Some of them who were employed by us to assist in certain operations in the ship, would dive in fifteen fathoms of water, and clear the cable, however entangled in the jagged rocks at the bottom.

I have heard from Mr. Young, that Tamahama, in the early part of his

career, being one day on board, requested of the captain an anvil, an article
of which he stood in great need. To
have a specimen of the spirit and skill
of the natives, Tamahama was told that
he should have one on the condition that
his divers should simply bear it up in
ten fathoms water. To this he instantly
agreed, and the anvil was thrown into
the sea. Tamahama immediately sent
some of his people down after it, expect-
ing to raise it without difficulty; but
they found it somewhat too heavy. Unwilling however to abandon so great a
treasure, they continued their efforts,
and, after long and repeated exertions,
succeeded in rolling the anvil along the
bottom of the sea, for about half a
mile, relieving each other alternately till
they gained the beach, and were received
by their countrymen with the loudest
applause.

These and similar exertions, although never declined by the divers, are often attended with dangerous consequences to their health. On their reappearing on the surface of the water, we observed their faces to be greatly swelled, their eyes red and inflamed, and blood discharging profusely from their nose and ears.

In a short time, however, they recover their usual state, and are ready to repeat the same exertion, and incur the same or greater injury. The only precautions employed by them on these occasions, are to close the apertures of the body, as if to prevent the entrance of the water.

To show their wonderful expertness in diving, they would sometimes go aloft to our top-gallant yard, then plunge into the water, pass under the ship's bottom, and again appear on the opposite side tumbling and sporting like so many water-fowl. We once attempted to turn this qualification to advantage, by employing some of the natives to nail parts of the copper sheeting on the ship's bottom. They would remain not less than three or four minutes under the water, come up to the surface to breathe, and return to their work. This, had we not witnessed, we should not readily have believed.

Both sexes are strong, hardy, and capable of enduring great fatigue. During our stay amongst them, the natives of Otaheite on board, struck probably with the lively manners of the people, and the appearance of the country, availed themselves of a dark night to slip down the ship's side, and swam unperceived to the shore. They soon however discovered that they were not in Otaheite; for in the Sandwich Islands none are permitted to be idle, but all must labour for a subsistence. This kind of life was not to the taste of the Otaheitans; they embraced the first opportunity to return to their native island, and arrived there soon after our return. With them likewise returned to Otaheite our carpenter, · who, as has been mentioned, had deserted from us a short time after we had reached the Sandwich Islands.

An intercourse between these islands and Otaheite may be of signal service to the latter island; as the natives of the former are well acquainted with the cultivation of the ground, and many other useful and ingenious arts to which the Otaheitans are almost entire strangers. Since the discovery of the Sandwich Islands by captain Cook, who so unfortunately lost his life on one of them (Owhyhee), the natives, who constantly lament his untimely fate, have made rapid progress in many mechanical arts;

and in the course of a few years more, they confidently hope to be in a condition to open a trade with China in vessels of their own construction, and navigated by their own people.

They are already well acquainted with trade on the north-west coast of America; and from thence they may draw many articles to make up their cargo for their own country, or the neighbouring islands to the westward.

It may naturally be asked, what articles of commerce or barter can be possessed by the Sandwich Islanders, a people just sprung from nature? The answer is at hand; they are able to furnish fire-arms, gun-powder, hardware, and cloth of different sorts; of all of which Tamahama has accumulated more than what is required for their own consumption.

These have been acquired in the exchange for labour and refreshments supplied to the shipping who have touched there; particularly such as are engaged in the trade to the north-west parts of America. When the cargoes of these last are completed, they readily part with such articles as remain at a very low rate, rather than be incumbered with them during the remainder of their voyage. Besides the above-mentioned articles of foreign introduction, the Sandwich Islanders possess the *sandal wood*, pearl oyster-shell, and some pearls, all articles of high value in the China market. One difficulty, however, still remains to their accomplishment of this object, which is their want of hands to navigate the ships on voyages of such length and intricacy. Fortunately however for these enterprising islanders, there are now resident among them several Europeans and

Anglo-Americans, men of ability and knowledge; such are Mr. Young, Mr. Davis, Captain Stewart, &c. &c. For twelve or fourteen years before our visit, these gentlemen had employed themselves successfully in instructing the natives, and their extraordinary chief Tamahama, in many useful arts, and particularly in that of navigation from island to island, so that many of the inhabitants have thus become brave, hardy, and not inexperienced sailors.

In the commencement of their trading expeditions, the Europeans would no doubt be entrusted with the command; but the islanders, from their ardour to learn, and capacity for instruction, would soon themselves be in a condition to take the charge of the vessels and cargo. It may perhaps be supposed that the king would be unwilling to entrust these vessels, property, and persons, to the Europeans and Americans residing among them, lest they should carry them to some distant part of the world, and then either wholly abandon them, or appropriate the profits to their own advantage. But of this there is little danger; as, independently of the good conduct hitherto evinced by these strangers, and their consequent good character in the islands, almost all of them have married in the country, and have a numerous offspring to whom they are powerfully attached, and have besides renounced all idea of ever returning to their native land.

This barter, or carrying-trade, between China and the north-west coast of America, would soon enrich the inhabitants of the Sandwich Islands, and their wants and desires for the luxuries as well as the conveniences of life would speedily increase; an opening would thus be made for the introduction of the arts, the manners, the improvements, and knowledge, of civilized Europe.

CHAP. XVII.

*Hint to the Missionary Society.—Departure
from the Sandwich Islands.—Passage to
the Southward.—Suspicious Behaviour
of the Natives.*

THE Missionary Society might perhaps
find it answer their purposes, to turn
their attention to that quarter where, in
my humble opinion, their benevolent efforts are more likely to prove successful
than in Otaheite. The Otaheitans are
indeed apparently softer in their manners than the northern islanders, but
they are far behind the latter in their
skill in the arts of life, and in their desire to acquire instruction of every kind.

Indeed, from certain events that took

place on their being discovered, and particularly from the lamented fate of the great Cook, the Sandwich Islanders have generally been regarded as a race of savage barbarians. The truth, however, is, as has been already noticed, that many of the horrible practices of the more amiable Otaheitans, such as infant murder, &c. &c. are unknown amongst them; and the fatal accident which befel Cook, is to this day deeply and generally deplored.

Their eager and insatiable curiosity to observe and understand whatever is doing by the Europeans, unrestrained by any of those considerations of propriety which influence civilized nations, has had a tendency to draw on them the character of rude and uncultivated men; but let it be considered, that this curiosity and ardour are not the effects of childish ignorance, but are produced by the most decided anxiety to learn whatever they see done: their seemingly rude behaviour will then be forgiven.

Should the Missionary Society adopt this hint, and make the experiment, I have no doubt that land might be easily procured as a grant or as a purchase. Tamahama is perfectly acquainted with the nature of a bargain, in the European sense of the term, and would conform rigidly to the conditions; differing in this, as well as in many other respects, from certain chiefs in Otaheite. The latter are constantly endeavouring to extort fresh remuneration from the missionaries there, whom they seem to regard only as strangers suffered to remain amongst them during their good pleasure.

Missionaries in the Sandwich Islands would moreover experience every aid from the resident Europeans. This is another great advantage over their countrymen in Otaheite, and Tongataboo. From the first arrival of the Otaheitan missionaries they were exposed to the greatest hardships and dangers from their own countrymen. Some desperadoes of Europe, at that time residing among the natives, instead of assisting these worthy men in their forlorn situation, they took a malicious pleasure in counteracting their efforts on all occasions, misrepresenting their views, and endeavouring to stir up the natives to outrage and violence. Young, Davis, and Stewart, would, on the contrary, be of infinite use in the Sandwich Islands; they would negotiate between the missionaries and the natives; and, being men of probity and character, in full possession of the confidence of Tamahama, their good offices could not fail of effect. I am persuaded that a simple application would not fail to secure their most strenuous efforts.

As a proof of the fidelity with which Tamahama fulfils his engagements, I may mention that of the cattle introduced by captain Vancouvre; the terms were said to be, that none were to be touched for a certain number of years. This condition has been rigidly preserved till that time expired, and these animals have in consequence become so wild, that none of the natives dare approach them. So that, ranging at their full liberty, they have destroyed the fences, trampled down the crops, and done much other damage. Though the inhabitants themselves have frequently suffered thus severely from their incursions, they have rigidly adhered to the condition of the original gift.

Owhyhee may be seen, in fine weather, at the distance of forty leagues out at sea; containing two very lofty mountains, Mouna Roa, and Mouna Kaa, whose summits are generally enveloped in clouds and vapours.

A few days before we left the bay of Karakakooa, seven spermaceti whales passed within half a mile of the ship, rolling along very deliberately to the eastward. Had any of our South Sea whalers been there at the time, there might have been excellent sport, and no very unprofitable employment; probably not less than two thousand pounds value for the day's work.

Having now accomplished the object for which we had visited the Sandwich Islands, that of laying in a stock of salt, we took in a sufficient supply of water; for this we were compelled to pay a most unreasonable charge, being obliged to employ the natives, as our own people would most probably have seized the opportunity of deserting.

In the evening of the 21st of January

1803, we weighed and stood away along the shore to the eastward. In this course we had a very full view of some eruptions from the volcanoes in the centre of the island of Owhyhee. With a favourable wind and clear weather, we briskly proceeded on our return to Otaheite.

On the 11th of February we made a small island called Mangee, which appeared very productive, as we observed on the shore a great abundance of cocoanut and bread-fruit trees. This island is probably well peopled, but as night was coming on, we had no communication with the natives. As the night approached, but before it was yet dark, observing several canoes employed in fishing, we hove to, in the expectation that they would approach; as further encouragement for them to do so, we showed them a number of lights fromthe ship, when, to our amazement, the whole shore was almost instantaneously illuminated, and this with as much regularity as if the intervals between the lights or fires had been carefully measured. No canoes however coming off to us, we made sail to the southward, being now considerably to the leeward of all the Society Islands.

In running across these seas, we fell in with several low islands, some of which, we have reason to believe, had never before been visited by Europeans. Such of the natives of these straggling islands as came within our observation, seemed to be an artful insinuating race; we found them at the same time to be both treacherous and barbarous. When we came near to these islands, the captain from curiosity went in the boat to have a near view of the country; but on reaching the shore, the natives gave such indications of artifice and cunning, that he did not think it prudent to land. They were all armed with spears and other offensive weapons. As the boat approached the shore, the women withdrew and retired up the country, a practice seldom used amongst savage nations but when hostilities are expected to take place. The captain however threw on shore a few nails and other trifles; and the natives in return sent off to the boat a few of the feathers of the Tropic bird, fastened to the end of a long bamboo.

These islanders were of a complexion darker by some shades than the natives of Otaheite; and much thinner and less cleanly in their persons. Their long shaggy hair was twisted together like a mat. The captain concluded that they must be very ill supplied with fresh water, as the highest part of the island did not appear more than six feet above the surface of the sea. Their chief food, as he supposed, must be fish and roots, as no bread-fruit nor cocoa-nut trees were to be seen on any part of the island.

We afterwards came to another island, having in the middle of it a large lagoon, which we could discover from the mast head. My curiosity prompting me to examine this singular spot, I went on shore, but found great difficulty in landing, as the shore appeared to be surrounded with a reef of rocks in every place, excepting towards the leewardmost end, where was a narrow channel not more than twenty yards across, through which the lagoon discharged itself into the sea.

Upon coming to this spot, the tide ran out so strong, that the boat could not stem the current; we therefore landed as near as was possible to this channel, and sent off two of the people, one of them a Sandwich Islander, to discover whether the island was inhabited. I remained with the others of the boat's crew on the shore, in the expectation of their return, but as they staid much longer than I had expected, I began to apprehend that some accident had befallen them. As the ship was near the land, I was in the act of putting off to her to procure some fire-arms, having neglected to bring any with us, when our two men made their appearance, and waded up to their necks to get to the boat.

I demanded of them if they had effected any intercourse with the natives, or had even seen any, for we had ourselves as yet discovered none. They said that they had seen and spoken with the islanders, and that they had strongly

solicited them to accompany them up
the country. As our men were both
without the spears which they had
carried from the boat, I enquired what
was become of them, and was informed
that the natives had made them understand by signs their wish to examine these
weapons; but when they had once got
them into their possession, they objected
to restore them.

Upon this information I resolved to
attempt to open an intercourse with
them, but as a necessary precaution returned to the ship for fire-arms; and
this being obtained, together with a new
addition to the number of my men, I
returned to the shore. Our two scouts
gave a very favourable account of the
natives, saying they appeared kind and
friendly. I therefore carried back the
Sandwich Islander, to serve, if possible, as an interpreter between the natives and me.

On our reaching the entrance of the channel to the lagoon, the tide had slackened so much that we were able to pull the boat against the tide. By so doing we got forward more commodiously than we could have done by land, as the ground was over-run with a thick underwood, which would have rendered our progress both tedious and irksome. By going on the water we were also out of the immediate power of the natives, who could neither surprise, nor mislead us, had such been their intention.

Upon gaining the inner end of this channel, we found the current no longer running outwards, but discharging itself into the lagoon with a rapidity equal to that of the Thames under London-bridge. The narrow inlet now resembled a mill-race; and we were so far engaged in it, that we had no alternative, but either to run forward through it, or incur the risk of being dashed to pieces on the coral rocks which lined the sides. In our way through this inlet the boat made two or three heavy plunges, which filled her more than half full with water; the helm lost all influence, and the eddy whirled us round with great rapidity. This anxious and hazardous situation lasted about two minutes, when at length we arrived without injury in the lagoon, and proceeded forward in quest of the natives; we expected that they would before this have again made their appearance, as they must have witnessed all our motions.

When we had advanced a short way, we discovered five or six who had left that part of the shore where we had first landed, and were moving up the country with all speed. Upon this I put the boat's head in shore, that I might if possible get before them, and thus effect an interview. The natives however, perhaps discovering our inten-tion, quickened their pace, as if they either dreaded or disregarded any such intercourse; and were a full quarter of a mile before us, before we could reach the shore of the lagoon. That they might not be alarmed at our numbers or arms, I landed only the two men they had formerly seen, who hailed them in the Otaheitan language and manner, to induce them to stop.

This at last produced the desired ef-fect, and our two men got up to them; the other two with myself still remain-ing in the boat, and following at a dis-tance. As our men on shore drew near, the natives again began to move for-wards, but so slowly that they were at last overtaken.

They now appeared to enter into

conversation with our two interpreters, one a native of the Sandwich Islands, and the other a sailor who understood and spoke fluently the language of Otaheite. This appearance of intercourse gave me great pleasure, as the natives would thus learn that our views in coming to their island were friendly, and might be advantageous. We continued at some distance in expectation of the signal to advance; but as no such signal was made by our people, and as they and the natives again moved forwards, I began to apprehend some ambush or other treachery on the part of the islanders.

The day was now declining, and we had been drawn a considerable way up the lagoon; we were moreover aware that, upon our return, we might be exposed to the same, if not greater dangers, as upon our entrance, and more particularly as it would be then dark : I therefore made a signal for our men to return to the boat, but, instead of obeying, they beckoned to us to advance.

Concluding that matters were now in a favourable way, we pulled up as fast as possible; and when we arrived abreast of them, our two men walked gently down to the water's edge, without saying a word more to the natives.

The sailor, on coming up to me, shook his head very significantly; and the Sandwich Islander said he believed the natives were canibals, applying his arm to his teeth, and showing as if he bit his flesh. It has been already mentioned, that on the first visit the natives had cajoled these men out of their spears; and on this occasion they had obtained their necklaces and ear-drops (the sailor being dressed in all respects like an inhabitant of Otaheite) The natives, to the number of eight, were all this time standing on the bank of the lagoon, apparently in doubt whether they should venture to approach us. In order to encourage them, I held up to their view some looking-glasses, knives, scissars, and sundry other articles; at all which they looked with great attention, but still remained unmoved. At last one of them ventured to come down to the stern of the boat, which now lay close to the land, ready to start, if necessary, at a moment's warning.

This man, who seemed to be the stoutest of the party, displayed a most curious mixture of fear and cunning, while he reached out one hand to receive a looking-glass in exchange for a pearl gorget which he held in the other. His manner gave me such a distrust of his intentions, that I thought it prudent to

secure myself by one hand to the boat,
lest in making this transfer he should
attempt to drag me out of it. This,
however, he did not venture, but made
off speedily to his countrymen with his
prize, the only one I have reason to
believe in the whole island.

Notwithstanding this man's sudden
departure, I continued to hold up as
before sundry articles, that might if possible induce more of them to approach.
None of them however showed any in-
clination to such intercourse, remaining
at a distance with a wild stare of amazement, not unmixed, as I thought, with
an air of artifice.

Had I been disposed to have inflicted
any punishment on these poor savages
for their treachery in plundering our
interpreters, it would have been easy
for us to have killed, or at least severely
wounded them, so that they and their

descendants would not have forgotten
our visit for many years. But compas-
sionating their ignorant and uncultivated state, and knowing that they were
not worse than all the other islanders of
the Pacific Ocean, I suffered them to pass
unpunished. Every act of theft is not
to be punished by shooting the offender
through the head. The great guns are
not to be discharged into a promiscuous
crowd upon every petty disturbance.
This is certainly as bad policy as it is
humanity; and if these people know
what murder is, it cannot much exalt
us in their esteem that we regard it so
lightly.

To shew them, however, that their
lives were in our power, even while
they remained at what they naturally
deemed a secure distance, I fired a
pistol in the air. The report frightened
these poor creatures so much that they

dropped down amongst the grass as if they had been really shot, and never attempted to move till the boat had been put off from the shore.

CHAP. XVIII.

Critical Situation.—Fortunate Escape.

So much time had been lost in these different proceedings, that I began to fear we should have some difficulty in finding our way out of the lagoon; we therefore made all haste back to the entrance, but it was dark long before we reached it, and we found ourselves involved in a vortex, which whirled us into a kind of channel somewhat beyond that by which we had entered; nor did we perceive our situation until, having proceeded about half-way along this channel, the boat took the ground.

Our people immediately jumped out of the boat, and tried to track her into the proper channel; no such passage,

however, could be found, for a-head the
boat was quite dry. We had, therefore, no choice left but to put back and
take a fresh departure, when in an instant we were again swept away within
the lagoon, and whirled round as before
with great rapidity. The tide, it seems,
had changed at the very time when we
were endeavouring to discover another
channel. We now found ourselves completely bewildered, as the tide made
up with such strength that it was impossible for us to stem it with our oars.
Our situation now became dangerous
and critical, and the greatest caution was
therefore necessary.

I made the people once more get out,
and track the boat along the edge of
the reef until we got to the top, which
terminated in a sharp point, and then
double the corner, by which means we
hoped to be free from the danger of

similar accidents. The men, equally anxious with myself, exerted themselves to the utmost; but the rocky reef on which they walked was composed of parts as sharp as flints, which severely injured their feet; and at almost every second step they found themselves up to the middle, often up to the neck, in the water.

It was now extremely dark, but fortunately we had discovered the ship's lights over the narrow belt of land between the lagoon and the sea; a sight which not only helped to keep up our spirits in these embarrassing circumstances, but to guide us in our search for a proper issue from the lagoon. The boat's crew continued, in spite of every difficulty, to drag her along the reef, until they could no longer endure the fatigue and pain of these arduous efforts. The tide had by this time begun to set into the lagoon in its greatest strength; for these reasons I judged it safest to bring the boat to anchor alongside the reef, setting up a land-mark to direct us in our course when the moon should rise, which we calculated to be about half past ten.

It was now between seven and eight o'clock, and the interval was beyond description distressing. We lay in a most perilous situation, surrounded with a savage race, suspected to be canibals. The imaginations of our people were filled with the most dismal apprehensions, and several began absolutely to despair of ever returning to the ship. It seemed indeed impossible that the boat should escape from the lagoon without being sunk or dashed to pieces; and if the crew survived such an event, they must doubtless have fallen into the hands of the inhabitants, never to be rescued.

In this manner had each his different opinion as to the fate awaiting us, but not one of us entertained any very sanguine hope.

At length the long-wished moon appeared, but half an hour later than we had reckoned, when we discovered ourselves to be about two hundred yards from the gut of the lagoon. Upon reaching this spot the tide was running gently. Turning the sharp corner of the reef, we immediately found ourselves in the proper channel, a relief for which our thankfulness is not to be expressed. Had the natives known our situation, and been disposed to take advantage of it, we might easily have been cut off, the channel by which we had returned being in its widest part not more than twenty yards across. But either they imagined us to have got off before it became dark, or had become afraid of

us from the discharge of the pistol. One
effect of this adventure was, that it considerably abated my ardour for enterprises of such a nature without previously making all due enquiries.

We passed safely through the inlet
to the sea, and within half an hour
found ourselves amongst our shipmates
on board, who had become extremely
uneasy concerning us.

Our two interpreters informed us,
that the natives of this island understood but very imperfectly the language
of Otaheite; but that they seemed to
have some notion of the existence of
such an island, which they supposed to
be ten times larger than its actual mag-
nitude. They had also a confused idea
of Pomarrie and his authority in Otaheite, and supposed him to be a person
of huge stature, in which they were
not entirely mistaken. How these de-

tached islanders came to have these no-
tions it is not easy to conceive; but they
may have been acquired from the natives of some other islands, driven
thither by stress of weather.

These lagoon islands are most striking instances of the infinite power and
wisdom of the great Architect of the
Universe; who has so arranged its materials, that the sea should be forced
from its proper bed, to make room for
the elevation of a narrow barrier to en-
close these portions of the deep. The
prospect of this very curious spot so
strongly affected me, that, whilst waiting for our people, who had gone up
the country, I involuntarily uttered a
kind of inward ejaculation, " How
wonderful are all thy works, O Lord,
and thy ways past finding out!"

This part of the Pacific has been
termed by navigators the *Labyrinth;*

and, I think, most properly, for the navigation is dangerous in the extreme. Here I cannot but observe, that had it pleased the great Architect of Nature in the plan of creation to have raised this part of the world but a few hundred fathoms from its present level, we should most probably have been furnished with countries of vast extent, and islands innumerable, which at present lay concealed but a short distance from its surface.

The ridge or narrow border of land surrounding the lagoon of this island, as far as I could observe, seemed in its broadest part to be only about two hundred yards across, in many places much narrower, and in no place more than eight feet above the level of the sea. No indications of the bread-fruit came within our observation, but here and there might be seen a dozen or more of cocoa-nut trees; half of them, however, were without tops, these having been probably broken off by the wind. I hence concluded, that it must at times blow very hard in this spot, for I never observed the same appearance in any of the Society Islands.

The lagoon, in the centre, seemed to be about six or seven miles across, and not less than twelve or fourteen in length; the whole interior being one continued sheet of water, and seemingly very deep. As we entered from the sea, we saw a canoe in it about two miles before us; it was paddling with all speed towards the shore: this was, most probably, to escape from us, as the people left it the moment they reached the land.

At the spot where we first touched, we found a few dried fish, sharks' heads, and two turtle shells, hanging up in a sort of maria, as an offering to the god of the natives.

There also, we saw a few miserable huts made of a kind of cocoa-nut matting, but saw none of the inhabitants, who had probably retired to a distance on seeing us land. In some places the ground was burrowed by certain animals, and part seemed to have been done that morning. The natives, as far as could be judged from our short intercourse with them, appear to be of the same race with those of the islands lying more to the eastward (wild and barbarous), who had been visited by the Captain; and some shades darker than those of Otaheite. Their appearance was loathsome and forbidding; and, excepting what subsistance they can draw from the sea and the lagoon, with a few cocoa nuts and roots, they seem deprived by nature of all other means of support. By what means they procure water we could not discover; and the population must of necessity be very scanty. We saw only eight natives all the time we were in the island. As far as we know, we were the first Europeans who had trodden this inhospitable spot.

At another island that fell in our way, far to the westward of the other, we were visited by about a dozen canoes, with one native in each. They brought off nothing for barter, but appeared to have been solely attracted by curiosity to survey the ship and people; no common spectacle in those parts of the world. They continued for some time near us, staring with wild amazement at every thing before them; but no endeavours on our part could prevail on any of them to come on board: we found, however, that their language was quite unintelligible to all our people. They accepted some of our trinkets, but seemed to set very little value on them. They were all completely in a state of nudity, excepting a small tuft of grass hanging down before the middle. Their countenance and manners had a very wild expression, and they were of a darker hue than any of the same race we had before seen; their persons were thin and meagre, their hair was thick and shaggy, and their bodies appeared to be covered with filth, and extremely forbidding. This island was a low, flat, sandy spot, like many others in this part of the world, having on it a few cocoa-nut trees, but giving few signs of any other vegetation. The food of the inhabitants must, probably, be fish, a never-failing article in the Pacific Ocean, with perhaps a few miserable roots, or other vegetable productions. It was our opinion that these islanders had never before seen any Europeans, otherwise they would have been more ready to court our acquaintance; particularly had they once known the use and value of the articles of iron manufacture, which they might have hoped to procure from us. The natives of such countries as were unacquainted with Europeans, I have constantly found to be shy, reserved, and very suspicious.

I cannot but here remark, that no skill in the navigator can reduce the navigation of these seas to any certainty of safety: the bottoms being so jagged, so irregular, and the inequalities of depths so frequent and sudden, that it is impossible to take any soundings which can be of much practical benefit.*

---

* For the situation of these islands, the geographical reader is referred to Mr. Arrowsmith's accurate map.

CHAP. XIX.

Visit the small Island of Matia.—Intercourse with the Islanders.—One of Pomarrie's Deputies exercising the supreme Authority.—Admiration of the Natives on seeing us pump the Ship.—Arrive the second Time at Otaheite.

FINDING no intercourse could be readily opened with these poor islanders, we made sail, and arrived at the small island of Matia, situated about fifty leagues to the northward of Maitea, which lies about twenty leagues east from Otaheite. Matia appeared to be as level as a bowling-green on the top, and might properly enough be called Table

Land. We found it was governed by a deputy sent by Pomarrie from Otaheite, being the most distant spot under his authority.

In this island lay a very large double canoe, which had left Otaheite six months before to collect tribute. The natives brought off to us abundance of bread-fruit and cocoa nuts, as articles for traffic, taking in return looking-glasses, nails, &c. &c. No hogs were produced, as the island furnishes very few, the principal support of the inhabitants being derived from the sea. In manners and appearance, the inhabitants of this little island bore a strong resemblance to those of Otaheite, but were less civilized; and our arrival excited amongst them a much greater degree of curiosity than had been shewn by the natives of the other islands we had just visited. The gorget, made of a pearl kind of oyster-shell, was universally worn; but their cloth, of which they produced some specimens, seemed to be much inferior to that of Otaheite. Many of the natives were dressed in a teboota made of long knotted grass, carelessly thrown over their shoulders, and descending to the knees. Their canoes, on the other hand, were superior in point of execution to those of Otaheite, being ornamented with a profusion of carved work.

We lay off and on in a very fine bay, under the lee of the island. The low land surrounding it, and extending to the hills, was rich in bread-fruit and cocoa-nut trees; and the beach, consisting of a fine sand, was crowded with natives, who watched all our motions with the most attentive curiosity. We admitted some of the chiefs, with their friends and attendants, to come on board the ship; they examined every object that presented itself to them with the most eager admiration. Having occasion at this time to pump the ship, the instant the water began to flow they were struck with amazement, and instantly left the quarter-deck to flock round the pump, showing an extreme inquisitiveness to know whence this water came, and how it was raised. Our mariner's compass next attracted their notice, and they seemed to be filled with astonishment when our Otaheitan chief on board explained to them its uses. He was listened to as an oracle of information, and told them many things, I believe, that at least bordered on the marvellous. He informed them that we possessed weapons, which, being merely pointed at them, would kill them in an instant; thus, no doubt, describing our fire-arms loaded. As far as we could learn, the natives had seen but one vessel before ours, which was probably a brig, as they represented her to have had but two masts.

Leaving Matia, we at length found ourselves restored to our old friends in Otaheite, where Pomarrie, Edeah, and Otoo, welcomed us in the most cordial manner. When these civilities were over, we were overwhelmed with applications for Sandwich Island cloth, and other articles of use or curiosity; and were quite unable to gratify the desires of our numerous applicants, who have no end to craving. They enquired the history of our voyage, and the wonders we had seen at *Popahie*, meaning *Owhyhee*. To these enquiries we gave the best answers in our power, and then presented to them a woman from the Sandwich Islands, brought with us in the ship on the following account.

In these remote parts of the globe we were often obliged to grant indulgences to our people, to which in other circumstances we should never have agreed, and which would never have been expected. Our second mate, a very useful person in the government of the ship's company, and in many other respects, pleaded hard with us, while we lay at the Sandwich Islands, to be allowed to carry a female native back with him to Port Jackson, in New South Wales. To such a proposition we would certainly have denied our assent; but, presuming on the importance of his services, the mate intimated that, unless his desire was complied with, he would leave us at the first opportunity.

Having already malcontents enough, without adding an officer to the number, and one who had such great influence with the men, we thought it most prudent to suffer him to bring this woman on board, and thus completely secured him to our interests. Much mischief might otherwise have been fomented in the ship, had he been irritated by a refusal of his request.

This person was passionately fond of his new mistress, and spared neither expence nor pains to equip her in the handsomest manner; she was, in truth, in a most woful plight when he received her from her relations, being brought to him without either wardrobe or jointure, but just as she stood, in her homely country dress. It was therefore necessary to clothe the poor creature entirely anew; no easy task in our ship, where we had neither mantua-maker nor linen-draper. Her husband, therefore, purchased seven purple-bordered shawls, on which, at every leisure moment, he worked in his best manner, until at length he produced a sort of long robe, stitched together rather than sewed. When fitted on the lady it had much the air of a leopard's skin, from the multitude of spots formed by the crossing of the coloured borders in all directions. That her finery might be of a piece, and she appear a little *à la mode de Britannie*, it was necessary she should wear pumps. The robe not only fitted, but quite delighted the poor girl, but with the pumps she would willingly have dispensed. It was her husband's will, however, that she should wear them, and she reluctantly submitted.

This was no small sacrifice on her part, for when the shoes were tied on, she moved as if she had been iron-shod. This was an operation too painful to be long endured; she therefore requested of her husband, that she might be unfettered; he consented, and her finery was

laid aside till she reached Otaheite. One
of her husband's shirts was substituted
for common wear, during the passage.

From the first moment of the ship's
arrival she was received with uncommon
attention by the ladies, who flocked
around her in crowds, regarding her at-
tentively from head to foot, and com-
plimenting her very courteously. Whether it was, that her colour so nearly
resembled their own, or that the splen-
dour of her dress so far surpassed any
thing they had before seen, they were
in raptures with her: every one pressed
eagerly forward to pay their respects.
After they had a while gazed at her in
this manner, the women withdrew with
her into the ship's hold. I know not
the object of this privacy, whether
that they suspected that she was some
man dressed up to impose upon them,
or that, previous to her reception

amongst them, there was a kind of masonry to be observed : so far is certain, that from what the woman afterwards said, they must have examined her very closely. None were more busy on this occasion than some of the branches of the royal family.

Every one was eager to become her Tayo ; perhaps, as she was the wife of an European, they cherished themselves with the hope that some presents might be in the way. They are in this respect most excellent calculators, but sometimes over-reach themselves, as was the case with respect to our armourer. She received many pressing invitations to visit them on shore, and complied with the greater part of them, dressed out to the best advantage. She did not, however, walk in her new pumps as if she had enjoyed the benefit of a dancing master.

CHAP. XX.

Death of the Father of Pomarrie.—Singular Character.—Departure of the Captain.—Residence in Otaheite Factory.

DURING our absence we found that the ship Nautilus had been at Otaheite, and taken away all the hogs she could procure. This was not the most pleasing intelligence.

Since our departure the father of Pomarrie had died, worn out by the gradual decay of nature, being blind at the period of his death. From his general character, he appears to have been a man of unexampled cunning and intrigue. Like many ambitious characters, he looked more to the end than to the

means; and contrived by various well
concerted schemes so to improve to the
advantage of his family the dissensions
of the island, as to procure the royal authority for his son Pomarrie. Tamarre,
son of the famous Oberea, the queen
in the time of Wallis, was thus deprived
of his right; and the family of Pomarrie invested quietly with the sovereign
power.

We found by this time that there was
no probability of procuring at Otaheite
any further supply of hogs; and that our
endeavours to this end required more
time than we could conveniently spare.
Dispatch was now our grand object. The
captain and myself therefore concurred
in opinion, that, as the most prudent
measure under our present circumstances, he should sail with the ship to some
of the islands to the windward, and
thence procuring a live stock of hogs,

should bring them to Otaheite to be slaughtered. Myself with two or three assistants were to remain at Otaheite on the salting business.

Upon the departure of the ship I was. received with transport as a temporary resident. I knew to what to impute this warm welcome; having brought from the ship a most plentiful store, I was richer than all the royal family of Ota-heite, and was received accordingly. For my greater convenience I endea-voured to render my temper as con-formable as possible to their manners and customs. From this cause I was never free from a crowd of all ages and sexes; and their curiosity was truly embarrass-ing. An Otaheitan must see every thing. By humouring them in these respects, I became a very general favourite; not only with the people, but with the royal family. Every one attended me with the greatest civility; and the king and myself almost daily exchanged presents and provisions. By these means our business of salting proceeded without interruption.

During this residence amongst them, I could not but observe their immoderate use of the ava. No sooner had they procured any fresh supply from Eimeo, or the more distant parts of their own island, than they gave themselves up to intoxication, and remained stupified for days together. I was again confirmed in my opinion, that the introduction of spirits would be attended with the general destruction of the population.

On leaving the ship, I requested the permission of Pomarrie to trade all over the island for hogs; this was most readily granted to me, as Matavia had become exhausted from the multitude of

its late visitors. As my salting business
required an addition of assistance, I was
compelled to engage some fugitive seamen, a kind of men whom I should
otherwise have rejected with disdain.. I
endeavoured at first to effect my purpose by means of the natives under the
superintendance of a European; and
sent them coasting around the island for
hogs; but the fatigue of the oars soon
.sickened them, and they could never be
prevailed upon to make a second trip. It
was truly ludicrous to see their yawns
and grimaces upon these occasions;
they would exhibit their blistered
hands, and exclaim most dolefully, Owhow, Owhow, Not good, Not good.
Indeed many of them never made their
appearance before me a second time, but
betook themselves to flight at the first
place where the boat landed. We might
have waited for pork till Doomsday be-

fore they would have acquired it for us by this labour. Our axes were good things, and our muskets better, but labour to an Otaheitan is always Owhow, Owhow.

From being a common dwelling-house, I converted my residence into a mansion, with more divisions and sub-divisions than all the other houses in Otaheite together. Immediately on landing, I partitioned off one-half for myself with a railing across, and a bar gate in the centre. This was for a while a sad bar to the Otaheitans. After a certain time I was persuaded to admit a few of them as an especial favour; all exclusion was henceforth at an end, they no longer troubled themselves to ask if their company was agreeable, but introduced themselves pell-mell, and *sans cérémonie*. Their only return for this impertinence, was an uninterrupted flow of compliments.

Opposite to me was a large trunk built for the purpose of keeping our pork; this furnished them with an ample theme: what a rich country must theirs be, which could supply such plentiful food for our half-starved countrymen! what a good thing it was for Prettanie that there was such a place as Otaheite, and such a man as Pomarrie!

The other half of the house I had set apart for our people, four in number, who immediately applied themselves to raising some large four-post bedsteads, all of which they hung round with Otaheitan cloth for drapery. Not one corner nor crevice of the house but was filled with natives; My tye, My tye, Good, Very good, resounded from every part. This flattery was very well calculated for our sailors, whose only aim was admiration; and our seamen being rich (that is to say, having me to draw on as their banker), were considered by them as very suitable objects of flattery. They accordingly gave them infinite credit for the elegance of their booths; and when called on to arbitrate, would take care to affront neither party, by pronouncing the booths of all equally inimitable.

Having learned from the Missionaries that a large stock of hogs might be procured from the windward part of the island, that part being too distant for the market of Matavia, I engaged some of the deserters whom I have beforementioned, upon this errand.

The condition of these men was by no means enviable: they complained very heavily, and with great reason, of the royal family; who, after having tempted them to desert their ship for the sake of their property, had left them when become poor to shift for themselves. They were now in the most abject state, differing little from a native; and many of them having no other clothes but the country marra. It required some manœuvring to manage these fellows; but by treating them in their own way, business at length proceeded to my wish. I moreover learned some intelligence of them, which much facilitated my purpose.

Their consequence increased with the wealth (wealth in Otaheite !) they procured by their labours; and, by their influence over the natives, they were of essential service. I never procured better nor cheaper hogs, than through the medium of these men. Other Europeans of the same class, seeing the flourishing state of their countrymen, were now eager to engage in my service; and, as the advantage was mutual, however little I liked them, I was induced to accept of their service.

I moreover learned from these Europeans some particulars with regard to the manners and customs of the Otahei-tans, which would otherwise have escaped me. These I shall take occasion to mention in due time.

The chief part of this business I en-trusted to Peter the Swede, he being the most experienced man in the island. I left it to his discretion to dispatch or detain the boat according as he judged proper, and as they found hogs scarce in one part of the island, they were in-structed to move to another.

Amongst my native servants, was a fellow recommended to me by one of the missionaries; he was sent with some of his countrymen to another part of the country to purchase hogs, and to home. There was now a true spirit of they were purchased, to see them with competition between the Europeans and the Otaheitans. I did not fail to en-

courage this as much as was possible,
and reaped the fruits of it by a most liberal supply of hogs. Our factory was
now a complete Exchange. With the
exception of the Missionaries, I had
every European in the island in my service; and had thus a better opportunity
of becoming acquainted with the manners and customs of the island, than
had perhaps before occurred to an European. What between the Missionaries
and the European deserters, I had the
means of hearing all sides of the question.

During the absence of the Swede, his
second in command was plundered of
his whole property; but, as Peter was
himself almost an Otaheitan in his
knowledge of the island, he easily
frightened the thieves into restoration.

CHAP. XXI.

Misfortunes of an Otaheitan Agent.—Characteristic Intercourse with the Royal Family.

THE native I had employed on the other part of the island, with his attendant hog-drivers, proceeded for a while in the quiet discharge of his business; but prosperity has spoiled many a better man, and the Otaheitans are not proof against it.

Being habited in some of my old clothes, he assumed the man of consequence, and in his plenitude of prosperity ventured even to take a wife. The women would not before deign him even a look; but he had now become rich, and therefore, in the language of Otaheite, as well as of other countries, Ta ta my tye, A very good man. That he might secure his domestic peace from invasion, and at the same time be uninterrupted in the discharge of his business, he brought his wife to the factory, and requested that I would not see him injured in his absence, as he did not seem to entertain the best opinion of her fidelity.

In the meanwhile, remaining on his station, he gave me much satisfaction by a diligent discharge of his duty. It was not so with the other Otaheitans, for they began to take mortal offence at his insolence and air of superiority. His pride was much increased by the circumstance of seeing himself at the head of so numerous a retinue of servants.

This foolish fellow at length received the merited chastisement of his folly.

His property was a temptation too great to be withstood by an Otaheitan; he was accordingly suddenly attacked, and plundered of all that he possessed.

His courage was so lowered by this misfortune, that he did not venture to make his appearance for two days; but at length stole away to the factory, and informed me of his misfortune. He was very desirous that I should avenge the injury by an invasion of the district. He repeated with great fervour, Ohow, ohow tata Otaheite, Bad man, very bad man the Otaheite man. I thought so myself, but excused myself from the invasion. I forgave him, and presented him with two axes. He wished me much to reinstate him in his former situation; but as they had begun with him, I thought the first loss the best, and I resolved to break up the encampment, as too near the frontiers. Captain

Main, the name by which he styled him-self as the Tayo of one of the missiona-ries, was now reduced to the humility and safety of a private station.

This gentleman paid me several visits afterwards. Harra way be anguny (Put away your anger), was his constant salu-tation on these occasions. He was the usual interpreter of the native language, and this one of his best specimens.

His wife was not very well pleased with this change of fortune; and think-ing she had married his wealth, and not himself, she deemed her contract an-nulled by this change of circumstances, and eloped without further ceremony. In the height of her husband's prosperity I had lent him a printed coverlid as a royal marra; his wife thought proper to take this with her. The poor fellow felt this misfortune more acutely than all his other mischances. I was so af-

fected by his complaints, and the ingratitude of the woman, that I requested
the interference of Pomarrie; but he
eluded me with his usual dexterity, by
the permission to arm my boat and invade the country.

Henceforth our business was wholly
conducted by Europeans. It was not
without the greatest difficulty that I
could keep a suitable check over these
profligates: the greater part of them
were from Botany Bay, and required
as strict a guard as the natives. It may
be thus readily conceived, that my situation was not the most enviable.

For the greater security against such
attempts, I put my property under the
care of the missionaries; whose house,
as compared with the best of the Otaheitans, was a perfect castle. Upon the
conclusion of a bargain, the natives es-
corted me in full procession to this ma-

gazine; and if the article purchased by them happened to be a musket, it was truly ludicrous to see the bustle and consequence which was made of it. The musket, handed from one to another, was examined minutely by all; and every one, finding some fault which had escaped the other, advised their country-men not to be imposed upon, but to insist on a good one. They were certain that this shot crooked, and that another would not shoot at all, and in this man-ner rejected some of my best pieces, and most usually remained content with the worst.

During this busy time, wholly occu-pied as I might be, I did not neglect a prudent attention to the royal family. They had much forwarded my business, by permitting my servants to range over the whole island in the quest of hogs; I therefore neglected nothing which could testify my grateful sense of their kindness. I sent them a daily allowance, as well for themselves, as for their voracious attendants, who, unless on the occasions of public feastings, have seldom an opportunity for these indulgences. My liberality procured me flattery and compliments in abundance. I have before observed, that they are never very sparing in this coin, when it answers any purpose.

This liberality, however, cost me less than they imagined; I sent them always the most indifferent parts of my hogs, such as I could not salt, and therefore, from the heat of the climate, could not have been kept. The most favourite part amongst the Otaheitans, the head, happened fortunately to be the most worthless part to me, and I had thus an opportunity of bribing them at a very inconsiderable cost.

Otoo used frequently to invite me, under one pretence or another, to attend him at his house; I usually found him loitering with all the indolence of an Oriental, and his queen as idle and vacant as himself. Upon these visits he pointed to the grass, as my seat, and throwing himself by my side, entered into familiar conversation.

Her majesty was equally condescending: she never failed, upon these opportunities, to rummage my pockets, and appropriate to herself whatever she might chance to find. The queen of Tiaraboo was equally troublesome, and examined me with equal care. After I had learned that this would be their constant practice, I usually carried about my person some trifling article, that the royal sisters might have the pleasure of pilfering it.

CHAP. XXII.

Outlines of the Royal Family.

I SHALL here throw together some observations, which regard the royal family, and the opinion entertained of them by the natives.

From the open and affable manner of Pomarrie, he is generally beloved by his own subjects. Whether this manner was natural or assumed, I do not take upon me to determine. It produced, however, its full effect, and caused him to be considered as the father of his people, though he had no wish so near to his heart, as that of fleecing them to the very skin.

This avidity, indeed, seemed common to every branch and member of the royal family ; Otoo was still superior in this respect to his father, and neither of them had any bounds.

Edeah had nothing of the affable and easy manners of Pomarrie ; she received the natives with an haughty deportment, and never descended to any thing like equality. It was much more dangerous to offend her than Pomarrie.

Otoo is a fickle, irresolute character, naturally formed to be the dupe of the sycophants by whom he is surrounded, and, as usually happens in such cases, his ill qualities are cherished to fuller growth by these very sycophants.

In a word, the general characteristic of the whole family is avarice. It is a subject of reasonable astonishment, to see the excess to which this passion is carried. Their stores consist of articles which they have received from the first visits of European ships, and which have rarely seen the light since they were first there deposited. Their hoards are never broken; their pleasure is to have, and not to enjoy.

I myself was once witness of a most notorious act of this unnatural, for thus I may call it, selfishness, in Pomarrie himself. One of the missionaries, an easy, good-natured man, had suffered himself to be wheedled out of the whole of what he possessed in the world; and, the clothes on his person excepted, had nothing left but a blanket. Pomarrie happened to meet this Good Samaritan at my house, and seeing that he had still this blanket left, attached himself to him, and contrived to get it. I remonstrated with Pomarrie upon this act of selfishness, representing to him the great need that he had of this relic of his former property, but all in vain; Pomarrie thanked him for the blanket, and, without further words, sent it to his store.

The only instance of generosity I ever experienced, or saw, whilst in these seas, was from the king of Attowaie, who supplied us with cocoa-nuts, salt, and vegetables, without stipulating as to price or conditions, sending on board all that we required, and leaving the remuneration entirely to us. I hope it is needless to add, that we took care that he should lose nothing by his generosity.

I had hitherto considered Pomarrie as an exception to his countrymen, but I now found that they were all of the same stock, and in species, as well as genus, all the same.

As my house was in some degree open, I suffered under a peculiar inconvenience; my premises were infested during the night by dogs, and their depredations on our pork were carried to some extent. As I knew the fondness of the Otaheitans for their dogs, I suffered for some time without complaint, but at length requested of Otoo, that he would command the natives in the neighbourhood, to keep their dogs at home; a request with which he not only complied, but added his permission to me to shoot any of them whom I should find hereafter trespassing. Availing myself of this indulgence, I had the misfortune to kill a favourite cur of the sister of Pomarrie, and another little dog belonging to the wife of one of the chiefs. This business caused great lamentation amongst the women, and for some time brought me into disgrace with them.

Edeah having to provide for a multitude of strangers, who had lately arrived from the Mottos,* was for some

---

* These will be more fully described hereafter.

time still more troublesome to us than the dogs. Our servants were native boys; she availed herself therefore of their services in secretly pilfering our pork. It was some time before I could discover by what means my stock was so visibly diminished, but at length having dismissed some of the boys under suspicion, and menaced others, I extorted their confession, that they had been employed by Edeah. They, moreover, showed me an opening formed by the removal of two pales under their bed, through which the stolen articles had been conveyed; and as the sides were greasy, there was no room for any doubt of their veracity.

I do not hesitate to say, that the whole island is but a receptacle of thieves. European property they will possess by some means or other; and theft they consider as a cheaper coin than they can

give by any method of purchase. They
will not hesitate to waylay and rob a
traveller; one method of theft is as pa-
latable to them as another. Pomarrie is
himself as dexterous a thief as any
amongst them, if borrowing, without
any intention of repayment, merit this
name. He would often request me to
lend him an hog, but if he once received
it, never again mentioned it. This could
be nothing but mere avarice, as he could
have had any number of hogs at a very
easy rate. But theft, as I have before
said, is a cheaper method of acquisition
than purchase.

To what is this general propensity to
be imputed? Theft, as an evil in itself,
and an evil intelligible to any one where
every thing is not in common, has
nothing to say to civilization; it should
be as intelligible to the savage, as to the
European. It is a violation of the law

of nature; a law before their eyes, and
legible in every circumstance of their
situation. There is therefore an honesty and dishonesty amongst savages,
as amongst the citizens of a civilized
country; and they are to be considered
as more or less depraved, accordingly as
they are more or less observant of this
elemental law of nature. The Otaheitans are thieves in every sense of the
word.

CHAP. XXIII.

Arrival of Paitia and his Sister.   Festivities on the Occasion.

ABOUT three weeks after the ship's departure, our friend Paitia returned from the Mottos. It has been before mentioned, that on our departure from the Sandwich Islands we left him on the brink of death; and that, as the last and only hope, he had been persuaded by his friends to go to the Mottos, to the end that he might be there weaned of his fatal passion for the ava. He now returned from this journey, and in every respect so much changed, that we had some difficulty to believe him the same. He was now stout, lusty, and plump; his skin, which was before scaly, was now fat and sleek, and his constitution appeared altogether renovated. Paitia was one of the brothers of Pomarrie, and being thus of the blood royal, had, as may be supposed, a numerous train of attendants in his retinue.

These Mottos are small sandy islets, almost level with the water-edge, and about twenty miles to the northwards of Otaheite. They abound with fish of every kind. Hither the Otaheitans and inhabitants of the neighbouring island resort in their summer excursions; these are their watering-places, and at those times the scene of noisy and general festivity.

Every thing was now hurry and confusion, to give a worthy reception to Paitia and his sister Awow. It was now a general holiday over the whole face of this part of the island. There was no discourse of which Paitia was not the subject. Gaming, feasting, and rioting, was now the sole occupation from the king to his meanest subject.

But the grand exhibition was to take place within an area of ground kept sacred to the use of the king, and an encampment was formed, that the king might see and hear the entertainment.

It was now a Bartholomew-fair time at Otaheite; nothing but singing and drumming from morning till night. It was usually mid-day before the sports began, or their natural spirits could scarcely have supported the fatigue. Their manner of wrestling is very singular; the party challenging places his left hand on the upper part of his right breast, and with his right hand strikes a smart blow on the cavity formed by the bend of the left arm; he is answered by his antagonist in the same manner, and the contest begins. Head and feet are equally employed upon this occasion, and the contest is terminated only when one of them receives a fall.

Those who were resident in the neighbourhood were usually opposed to the strangers. Our Europeans, in general, had no chance with them; but the moment one or the other received a fall, the contest was at an end, and their threatening looks and ferocity changed into smiles and affectionate salutation. The temper of the Otaheitans is, in this respect, very amiable; they appear absolutely incapable of malice, and if we adopt an epithet from poetry, we may truly call them " a land of gentle souls." One contest, however, was no sooner decided than another party came forward, and this continued upwards of a week.

Nor were these sports confined solely to the men; the women were equally emulous to signalize themselves, and their feats of pugilism were equally honourable to their courage. They fought with equal resolution and dexterity, hanging on each other's necks like bull-dogs, tearing their hair, bumping the stomach of each other, both with their heads and feet; in a word, neglecting no means of victory. Their husbands and relations were spectators of their efforts, and encouraged them to continue them; upon one or the other of them receiving a fall, the affair was terminated, and the parties, after adjusting their hair, would tenderly embrace, and be as good friends as ever.

The Arreoys were peculiarly active in exciting the parties upon these occasions. After having spent the greater part of the afternoon in this manner, we were always entertained in the evening by an heva, or dance. The women, to the amount of ninety or an hundred, formed themselves into two circles, one of them consisting wholly of the residents, the other of the strangers, and each with their separate band of music. It is impossible for me to describe the variety of sounds produced by them, by the simple means of the exhalation and inhalation of their breath, for with the exception of a few words chaunted at the beginning of a song, they made use of no words, but tuned their throats so as to produce a variety of tones, and all of them in perfect concert.

In truth I was astonished at the exact union, regularity, and good time. The king, looking over my head, would frequently demand of me how I liked the entertainment, and whether we had any thing which could equal it in Prettanie. I have before said that their dances have been mentioned as replete with obscene motions ; but I saw less than what I had been led to expect. If the very origin of dancing, according to some, was in the imitation of what is not fit to be mentioned, the Otaheitans have now become so civilized, that the coarseness of the resemblance is now worn off.

The men also had their part in this entertainment. About one hundred and fifty young fellows were so seated in' two rows as to form an avenue between them about seven feet apart ; they then chaunted, and inhaled, and exhaled, in the same manner as the women, who had but now finished. The motions were as cotemporaneous as those of one man; nothing could be more accurate. The king frequently interrogated me in the same manner, and I gratified him by the same answer, that all I saw was admirable, and that we had nothing like it in Britain.

Before the assembly broke up, some stout muscular young fellows came forward and endeavoured to amuse the assembly by exhibiting some obscene attitudes. They were received however with very cold encouragement. I am of opinion that this favourable change in their national taste, is to be imputed to the exertions of the missionaries. Would to heaven that their efforts might prevail to induce these savages to cease from the practice of infant murder, and human sacrifices!

The Arreoys appeared to me to have the conduct of the whole. During the whole course of these entertainments, the music seldom stopt one moment. Our house and stock-yard were during all this time crowded with natives; nothing exempt from their scrutiny, as it was a point of hospitality to shew every thing to the strangers.

Being at length, and with difficulty, satisfied what was this thing, and what was that, and what the use, of every thing they saw, they would run to their fishing seine. This is a net made of the leaves of the cocoa-nut tree, and extending full a quarter of a mile in length; it will sweep round a rock without much injury, and whatever fish may be adhering to its side, will force from their holds without difficulty. Some of the king's attendants are always in waiting upon these occasions, and seldom fail to seize upon two-thirds as the royal tribute. The king being thus served, the multitude are let loose upon what remains, a scene truly ludicrous: a general scramble of men, women, and children, then ensues; the seine is usually torn to pieces in the contest; every one then decamps with his prize.

These amusements continued during the whole week after the arrival of the illustrious strangers, but slackened towards the end; the country people returning to their homes to prepare for the repetition of the same merriment in their own district.

When any of the greater chiefs return from these mottoes, as they are called, they never fail to make the circuit of the whole island. Their retinue is then numerous, for simple as is their life, they are not without a taste for pomp. Their followers consist of all the strangers from the mottoes, and the same merriment and diversion continues wherever they stop; add to this, they are every where loaded with presents; so that by the time they have made the circuit of the island, a peregrination which usually occupies them three months, their canoes return as rich as a fleet of galleons. Their connection with the royal family renders the people more than ordinarily liberal; it is moreover the custom of the country upon such occasions, to hold no bounds in their generosity.

These motto excursions, or royal progresses, have doubtless no other purpose, than of extorting from the liberality of the people these voluntary taxes. Nothing indeed can exceed the prodigality of the people, except it be the avidity of the chiefs.

The conclusion of this hurricane of riot and confusion was to me a moment of satisfaction; for however little interest, and whatever little the part which I bore in this festivity, no inconsiderable share of its inconvenience fell upon me. Our house was situated in the midst of a plantation of cocoa-nut trees, and was surrounded with a railing in-

closing about half of an acre, where we
had erected a blacksmith's shop, and a
boat-house. The circuit of this inclo-
sure became a general mall; and during
the time of the feasting, the natives
were constantly introducing their
friends the strangers, to see the armourer at work. They would express
their admiration of his ingenuity; but
the fellow knowing with whom he had
to deal, and little moved by their flattery, contrived by plentifully scattering
his sparks, to keep them at a respectful
distance. And this management was
necessary for more reasons than one;
for independant of their wearisome impertinence, and constant interruption,
nothing was safe within their reach. If
any of our hogs made their escape, they
seldom failed to change masters; and
after having been detained some time,
have not unfrequently been again

brought to us, and a second time offered for sale. Their impudence of theft
indeed exceeds all belief: an English
horse-dealer might here add much to his
proverbial dexterity.

The missionaries have suffered much
from this national breach of the eighth
commandment; a strayed hog is never
recovered. Their goats are safer, for
the aversion of the Otaheitans to goat's
flesh is invincible.

Notwithstanding their many and daily opportunities to improve themselves
in the mechanical arts, the utility of
which they daily observe and confess,
it is incredible to perceive their slow advances in this knowledge. With one-
half of these advantages, the Sandwich
Islanders would have made a very different progress. In the whole island I have
only seen two men who could work even
tolerably in iron, though Pomarrie has a

forge and bellows, and a complete blacksmith's apparatus. Two or three of them
alone know even how to handle a saw,
and scarcely one who knew any thing
of any other carpenter's tools. They
seem to prefer having their work done
by us, to doing it by their own industry. It would seem natural to imagine
that the beauty and evident utility of
the missionaries' garden, would operate
at once as a stimulus, and an example.
But to whatever cause it is to be imputed; whether to the natural fertility of
their soil, which renders industry needless, or to the physical effect of a climate producing an irresistible indolence;
this has not happened; and the Otaheitans will be yet many years without
these elements of civil life, the common
working of wood and iron.

During a heavy gale from the westward, a canoe arrived at Otaheite from

Tapeyomanna, on a political mission to Pomarrie.   The chief of this embassy took frequent opportunities of visiting our factory, and was particularly solici- tous, that on the return of the ship we should pay their island a visit.   At this time we also received frequent visits from two chiefs of the island of Bola- bolla, one of them said to be uncle to the reigning king, who were equally importunate with our other friends. Fire-arms and powder were their object; they would have scrupled at no price to have obtained them; it was their souls' desire; if they had it, they would have made no scruple to have placed an equal quantity of gold in the opposite scale against a musket.   These men enjoined the strictest secrecy in their interviews with us, lest Otoo should betray them to the Uliteans; and to guard against any attempt of this nature, were very urgent to be accommodated with a passage on board our vessel, against his return. The royal family had, doubtless, some deep political motive in suffering these men, the implacable enemies of the Uliteans, to procure muskets by barter with the ships. This motive, however, I cannot profess to conjecture.

The propensity which these people have to continual wars with each other, is of the most fatal consequence to the happiness of these islanders. Their minds have thus acquired a ferocity, which otherwise seems not natural to them; but, notwithstanding this seeming fierceness, I am persuaded that a few determined Europeans would find no difficulty in subjugating them. As an instance of this, I shall here introduce the following circumstance.

The Swede whom I have before mentioned, had obtained permission to trade

for me all over the island, and from this
indulgence had taken the liberty of introducing himself into the districts hos-
tile to Pomarrie. These people gave
him a most welcome reception, having
formerly felt the effects of his prowess,
when fighting the battles of Pomarrie.
In these wars he had killed many of
their countrymen; for, being a courageous fellow, he always took the
lead upon these occasions. They now
held out many flattering proposals, if he
would reside amongst them; they promised that he should have hogs, houses,
lands, and canoes.

The Swede had already experienced
the ingratitude of the opposite party;
for he had no sooner accomplished their
purpose, and by his efforts perhaps saved
Pomarrie and the king, than he was
laid aside as a tool no longer wanted.
He had thus very reasonably become

dissatisfied with them; and thinking
that he had no very particular obligation,
or any duty of allegiance, he resolved to
change masters, and the opportunity
now presented itself. He thought that
he might place more dependance upon
his new than his former employers. He
brought to our house whatever property
he possessed, to be conveyed thither the
next time our boat should go that way,
which, until this event occurred, I
proposed should be on the morrow.
But when he made the request, that
himself and family, four in number,
with two others of the people whom I
had discharged, should be conveyed
thither, I thought it a duty that I owed
my countrymen the missionaries, to inform them of his purpose.

Alarmed at the probable consequences
of this event, some of them strenuously
requested me to remonstrate with him,

and if possible induce him to lay aside this purpose. Some of them expostulated with him, but to very little purpose; he was seemingly resolved to persist in his own way.

In answer to their reasonings, he complained very heavily of having been so often deceived by Pomarrie; and that, though he had not relaxed one moment in his efforts to advance the interests of Pomarrie, the ends of the latter were no sooner effected, than his promises were forgotten, and his reward denied or eluded. This was indeed very true; the poor fellow, after all his services, was sometimes hard put to it for a subsistence.

The missionaries had no answer to this, but to request him to delay the execution of his purpose, till they should have exerted their interest with Pomarrie, and procure him some redress. After some further negociation, I was appointed mediator between the parties.

In the mean time Pomarrie, being informed that he was about to lose, and his enemies to gain, so stout a warrior, hastened in terror to Matavai, and requested me to interpose, and procure a reconciliation. The Swede was sullen and determined. He turned a deaf ear to all that Pomarrie had to say.

I now began my part: taking Pomarrie aside, I informed him that all my negociations with the Swede had been fruitless; that he had a heavy and just cause of complaint; that he was exasperated by neglect, after the services of so many years; that having done so much for him, he certainly merited some permanent return. Pomarrie demanded what he now wanted? I replied, a sufficiency for himself and family. Pomarrie was eager for delay, under the pretext of the necessity of consideration, as every place would not alike suit the Swede.

About this time Edeah arrived, and began in her usual way of blandishment, reminding the Swede of their former relationship; for, in his first marriage, he had married a relation of the royal family, and had in consequence a large tract of land assigned him. But the Swede was as inexorable by her as by Pomarrie.

Here again I was referred to. To which I replied, that unless something was done, and that without further delay, for his satisfaction, my interference would be useless, as he was determined that he would no longer be the dupe of his confidence in their promises. The royal pair requested, that I would not suffer his property to be removed till the morning, when they would meet me again, and arrange something to his satisfaction.

The missionaries concurred in this request, equally anxious that every thing should be arranged. In the evening I spoke to him again on the same subject, and went still farther than I had done before, advising him to think seriously before he acted, and not to persist in a determination which would effectually remove him from the island; that the interest of the missionaries was a thing of too much consequence to be exposed to any risk, and that therefore, should he execute his intention, and by joining the enemies of Pomarrie, endanger their safety, he might rest assured he would be removed upon the arrival of the first missionary ship, and forcibly reconducted to Europe. I knew that this representation could not fail of due effect, as of all things he dreaded nothing more than leaving a place where the necessaries of life were certain. His disease moreover, the elephantiasis, rendered it impossible for him to live by his industry in any of the kingdoms of Europe; this he knew well, and therefore dreaded any removal. Whether he understood my policy, or from any other cause, he listened to my remonstrances with callous indifference, affecting at the same time to be much obliged to me for my interference. He had indeed profited much by his long abode amongst these islanders, his natural cunning having been much whetted by their example. Pomarrie for once kept his word with unusual exactness; he was early with us the next morning, and pointing out a lot of land, about half a mile distant from our residence, said the Swede might take possession of it, and that shortly he would do something better for him. Opposite to this lot of ground was a small island; Pomarrie added, that the fish around this islet should be his sole property, and that next day he would accompany him to perfect his investiture. The Swede was satisfied so far, but still harped on the ingratitude with which he had been long treated. Next day Pomarrie again visited us, and the parties departed; the business was adjusted, and every thing, to all appearance, reconciled.

I am of opinion that this business was prevented in time, as had the Swede once settled among the Hidieams, the consequences must have been fatal, as well to the greatness of Pomarrie, as to the safety of the missionaries. The Swede would have proved a most dangerous enemy, being as artful as courageous. He would moreover have formed a kind of rallying post for all the runaway seamen, and other discontented

Europeans on the island; he was in every respect formed for the head of a low party,* and his desertion to this people would most probably have produced a series of fatal wars.

In the last grand attempt against the Attahourans, this man led the van, and through his still steadily adhering to the cause of Pomarrie, and the assistance of our people, there is little doubt that the Attahourans were much more easily intimidated than had the case been otherwise. Through his generalship in the preceding war, in 1802, they had lost many of their people; for, whilst the Attahourans were wasting their time in

---

* What made him much more dangerous at this time was, that I had discharged the renegadoes I had employed on first landing. These men being now utterly at a loss how to dispose of themselves, would willingly have joined the same party, which would have thrown a wonderful preponderancy in the opposite scale. Nothing but the fear of such consequences could have induced Pomarrie and Edeah to have made such concessions as they did to this man.

the enemy's country, this man, being of a ferocious and sanguinary disposition, made a sudden irruption into Attaboyra with a party of Pomarrie's adherents, and put many to death : the objects of his vengeance were principally old men, women, and children.

In all cases of emergency, this fellow had been looked up to as a deliverer; having, shortly after becoming a resident, with a small number of Pomarrie's warriors, reduced to obedience a whole district, which had thrown off their dependence on Otoo. At the time of the missionaries settling in Otaheite, he had acted as interpreter between the chiefs and missionaries; and during the Duff's voyage to the Friendly Islands and Marquesas, had accompanied that ship thither, to give them every assistance in his power; which, from his long residence amongst the natives, was, as may be supposed, very considerable.

CHAP. XXIV.

Long Absence of the Ship.—Melancholy
Intelligence of her Fate.—Narrow Es-
cape of the Crew.

However I might keep my feelings to
myself, I had been for some time very
uneasy with respect to our ship, as it
had now been absent two months instead
of three weeks; the latter period being
the utmost I had allowed for her long-
est possible absence. The people with
me were equally alarmed and less dis-
creet; they had already begun dream-
ing, and it was not without much
difficulty that I could ridicule them out
of their interpretations. I readily acknowledged that the vessel had been ab-

sent much beyond the expected period of their arrival; but imputed this absence to the prevalence of the westerly winds, which most probably had driven the ship to the eastward. They were still however persuaded, that from the long delay something had happened; and to confess the truth, I had begun to entertain the same opinion. At length the fatal remains of the Margaret were discovered by the natives, about three leagues to the northward of the island. The conjectures of the royal family, the missionaries, and the natives, seemed all to lead to one point; and by their expressive looks at me, it was not difficult to comprehend their object. The sight of the sail confirmed me in my apprehensions beyond any further doubt; it was as large as three of our boat's, and could belong to nothing but a ship. The king and missionaries demanded my opinion, but I was too much moved to express my sentiments. Some canoes coming across from the Mottos at this time, Otoo and myself walked up to them and made new enquiries, but they were equally at a loss with ourselves; some asserting it to be a boat, others a ship. By this time a gun was fired, on hearing which I immediately launched two canoes, and (whoever they might turn out to be, for I had now again begun to hope) sent them to their assistance. They returned but too soon, with the intelligence that the remains were those of the Margaret converted into a punt. The crew of the punt had been for the two last days on an allowance of two wine glasses of water *per diem.* The canoes therefore again hurried back to the relief of my unhappy comrades.

The punt however, having been built

square, from their having been unable
to bend the planks, could only sail before the wind ; and instead of reaching
Matavia, had much difficulty in making
the most leeward part of Otaheite. Had
they missed this, they must to all appearance have inevitably perished ; for
within an hour afterwards the wind
blew a tempest, accompanied with thunder and lightning, and torrents of rain,
during the following night. Pomarrie,
much to his credit, no sooner heard of
their arrival, than he hastened to their
assistance, lest the enemy should avail
themselves of their weakness, and plunder them of the little which they had
yet left. He got a hog and bread-fruit
roasted, and spared nothing to alleviate
their sufferings ; sleeping in the house
during the night to prevent thefts.

Having left the factory under the
charge of the missionaries, I had by

this time joined my comrades. Pomarrie was chiefly alarmed, lest we should
be attacked by the Attahourans, being
in their immediate neighbourhood. Had
this attempt been made, wearied and
worn out as were the crew, it could not
scarcely have failed of success. The
tempestuous state of the weather was
moreover peculiarly favourable for
such an enterprise.

Fortunately however, the fears of the
king and ourselves were altogether
groundless. Had the crew been compelled to put in at any other island, I
am persuaded they would have been
plundered; and that their distress would
have produced no other effect, than that
of animating their enemy to greater exertions, in proportion as the possible resistance could have been so feeble.
There is little generosity to be expected
in any intercourse with a savage enemy;

they know and acknowledge nothing of what a civilized nation calls the point of honour. To be defenceless among them is to be but an easier prey; an enemy over whom a victory is certain, and the danger of the contest nothing.

Pomarrie did not forget a few days afterwards to demand his presents. It was not so with the missionaries; there was no selfishness here; they were animated by no other impulse, but that of christian charity, which extends its arms to the miserable, and binds up the broken reed.

Being too fatigued and worn out, the crew were unable to attend divine service in the chapel of the missionaries: Mr. Jefferson, therefore, with that anxious piety which distinguishes him, preached a thanksgiving sermon in the house.

CHAP. XXV.

*Particulars of the Ship during its Absence.
—Ill Conduct of the Sailors.*

IT may be imagined that our first enquiries, after the sense of our loss had in
some degree subsided, were directed to
the circumstances of this misfortune.
These circumstances, as reported to me
by the Captain, were as follows: · · ·

From contrary winds, and lee-cur-
rents, the ship had been a fortnight in
getting to the windward, and it was
only the day previous to the accident,
that he had commenced trading with
the natives. On the morrow, with the
mutual satisfaction of both parties, the
trade was to be renewed, but according

to the old and often verified adage, man contrives, but God executes. The business of the captain, as he proposed to renew the trade on the succeeding morning, was to keep his station during the night; but whilst in the act of plying to windward for this purpose, the ship was unfortunately lost on a low reef of rocks and sand-banks. Being almost on a level with the water's edge, they had never before been discovered. The captain and the crew landed without much difficulty, and employed themselves in saving whatever stores were within their reach; but during the ensuing night the boat was stolen through the treachery of the Otaheitan natives, nor were they ever afterwards enabled to recover her. Nor had these wretches been satisfied with this plunder; for, together with the boat, the muskets and ammunition, with which they had been

provided to defend themselves against
the attacks of the natives, had disap-
peared, and scarcely an hope of safety
was left.

It was necessary, in the first instance,
to build another boat from some planks
on board the vessel: this they commenced without loss of time, and had
almost completed it, when the natives
of the neighbouring islands began to collect in vast numbers, and annoy them
exceedingly; their situation was truly
dismal.

However, by force of unexampled exertion, and unremitting vigilance, they
contrived to repel these attacks. The
boat was at length finished, and every
thing in readiness to quit this unfortunate
spot. Their misfortunes, however, were
not at an end; after repeated trials it was
now found impossible to get the boat
over the reef, and it was necessary to

abandon this hope of escape. The misery
of their situation was now redoubled;
their spirits, and powers of labour, were
exhausted, and their planks and nails
expended in building the boat.

Necessity is the mother of invention.
Every one was not only allowed, but
called upon, to deliver his opinion as to
the best means of safety and escape. The
natives were hourly becoming more and
more troublesome; not a day passed without some skirmish with these savages.

Something, however, was necessary
to be done; as their last resource, therefore, the deck of the ship was broken
up, and with the boards and nails a kind
of punt was made. Being flat bottom-
ed, it of consequence floated in less
water, and with some difficulty was got
over the reef.

They did not, however, escape without some cost. Whilst the punt was in

preparation, the savages during the night attacked the two sentries, and pierced them with their spears in a manner which, but for the uncommon natural strength of the men, must have terminated in their immediate death. The bowels of one of them hung out when he was delivered into the hands of Mr. Elder, the surgeon of the missionaries at Otaheite. His life was long despaired of, nor could he possibly have survived, had he experienced less kindness and attention. And here let me not forget Mr. Jefferson; but to say every thing in one word, I shall only add, that he practised actively what he preached zealously. Once for all, I must express my regret, that such labourers are fixed on so ungrateful a soil: may their future harvest be such as to reward their toil!

Such was their situation when the punt was finished. Spent with fatigue;

and still more with anxiety of mind,
and perpetual alarm, they became weary
of life, and whatever might be their future fate, implored the captain to leave
the rock. It was in vain for the captain
to remonstrate; they exclaimed unani-
mously, that they would rather perish
by the craziness of their punt, than
wear out a lingering existence on the
rock, or be cruelly murdered by the
savages. It may not be unnecessary here
to observe, that two out of three of
these fellows were convicts; and however courageously they had dared the
laws of their country, they were here
only remarkable for their pusillanimity.—
The craft being finished, they em-
barked to the number of eighteen, having on board only a few muskets, a small
quantity of powder, one bag of bread,
and ten gallons of water. Even this was
so brackish, that nothing but their pre-

sent situation could have induced them
to have made use of it; for the sand-
bank not being more than forty yards
across, and not more than four feet above
the level of the sea, it was only by dig-
ging a good depth that any could be
obtained.   The water oozing through
the sand, was in some measure purified
from its saline qualities.   The natives
must, to all appearance, suffer much
from this want.   Scarcely were they on
float, after leaving the wreck, when the
savages rushed on board, and tore open
and took away every thing portable.

After a voyage of five days, in this
most miserable of craft, they at length
reached Otaheite, nearly exhausted. We
now experienced the truth of a maxim,
which history in events of greater consequence has too frequently verified;
how much authority sinks under ill
success.   During the whole of the ship's

absence, the business of salting pork at our factory proceeded perfectly to my satisfaction, but this reverse threw every thing into confusion; so universal is the influence of fortune; so impatient are we of restraint; so willing to avenge ourselves of a temporary superiority, and to gain a triumph over our former masters.

Not content with this temporary triumph, these miscreants most effectually prejudiced the minds of the natives against us, by alleging that the loss of the vessel had brought us all upon a level, and that to continue any longer in our service was to work for employers who had no means of making them a recompence. Under this impression the native boys, who before had courted our service, withdrew from us in disdain, and attached themselves to these desperadoes.

In · a word, the captain and myself were now left to shift for ourselves, for the fellows took themselves off, and seemed pleased with the idea that their masters would be much embarrassed by their desertion. This conduct was the less pardonable, as the greater part of them had in fact nothing to do, having native servants to perform all the drudgery, and the care of clothing and providing them falling wholly upon me. It was not many days, however, before they discovered their mistake; it has ever been found as happy as extraordinary a trait in the character of this kind of people, that they grow as soon weary of their mutiny, as they had formerly been of their good conduct.

They at length assembled in a body corporate, and made a regular demand of the muskets and powder saved from the wreck; a demand to which I strongly objected, as peculiarly unreasonable in our present situation. Mr. Jefferson, one of the missionaries, having received a commission of the peace from the governor of New South Wales, I referred the claimants to this gentleman, and consented, upon my own part, to abide by his decision. To this they accordingly agreed, and we appeared before Mr. Jefferson about three o'clock the same day. Fearing as well for the peace of the island as for that of his mission, Mr. Jefferson pronounced an absolute negative upon their demand of the muskets. We offered them other articles; some were contented, others murmured. The most troublesome of them were such as had saved some property, however little valuable, from the wreck: these were considered by the natives, and therefore considered themselves, as

wealthy men, men of no small consequence.   There was something peculiarly ludicrous in the insolence of these
fellows, and almost equally so in the artifice with which the natives encouraged
their ideas of their own importance.
The end of it was, as might be imagined,
their property gradually vanished, and
with it the uncommon attention of the
natives ; and the fellows, become poor,
returned to their duty, and their common sense.   The stage of life does not
present a broader farce, than that of a
low man elevated into sudden and unexpected consequence.

I know not how it happened, but if the
natives acted as leeches to these fellows,
the royal family were the final channel
to which the stream found its way.   By
some means or other, the king and Pomarrie were ultimately in possession of

the whole of their property. This was no inconsiderable addition to their royal exchequer, and, I make no doubt, will long be considered as a fortunate æra in the Otaheitan treasury.

With some difficulty, I at length effected their general return to their duty. I have no doubt that they had been led to the demand of fire-arms and powder by the artifice of the chiefs, who knew very well that they were a kind of spunges, and that, once filled, they had only to squeeze them to get to themselves what they contained. Their riches gone, our fellows began to experience that new friends are the same in Otaheite as in most parts of the world. The richest man in Otaheite is always the man of most importance; and as I had saved something, my consequence returned, whilst that of our troublesome crew vanished with their property. I was now once more, Pomarrie; that is to say, not unworthy of being the Tayo of the king.

CHAP. XXVI.

Voyage to Eimeo.—Occurrences in that Island.

WE had now seen enough to know that the very comfort of our stay at Otaheite depended on our being able to pay for it. The apparent generosity of these people is but another kind of policy, a cunning artifice, under the cover of which they were more readily enabled to dupe us. There was another circumstance moreover which much embarrassed us: Otaheite within the two last years had become so well supplied with European articles, that they had now become very difficult; and as our stock was now rendered by our wreck very limited, we were not unfrequently at a loss to keep up the market.

These circumstances concurred to induce a resolution to make a trial of one of the neighbouring islands, and Eimeo was fixed upon for that purpose. As fewer ships had touched at this island, I concluded that indifferent property would here find a more certain sale. Hogs moreover were said to be here more numerous.

Our passage over was very rough; and the sea being heavy, and the wind fresh, we narrowly escaped being swamped upon reaching Tallow harbour. Having taken nothing with us, we were in great want of refreshment, but could procure nothing to eat; the greater part of the natives being absent about a mile distant up the harbour, entertaining a travelling gang of Arreoys and strangers from Otaheite. From our situation, we could distinctly hear the drums and noise. None, or at least very few of the natives, came near us during the night; and we began to repent that we had left our factory at Matavai.

In the morning, at sun-rise, we ran down inside the reef with the purpose of procuring better quarters. The water being shallow, our people were not unfrequently compelled to leave the boat and drag it for miles. As they had no food, and were already sufficiently fatigued, they did not bear this with a very exemplary patience. I encouraged them to perseverance, and promised them provisions if they could be procured at any price; but with all our efforts it was near eleven o'clock before we reached a house, or any thing in the shape of a house; and in the islands of Otaheite and Eimeo, to reach a house is not always to find food. A few mountain plantains, two or three heads of bread-fruit, and a small pig, were all that we could procure. We should doubtless have fared better, had it not been for the Arreoys; but wherever these gentlemen come, they seldom fail to clear the coast before them.

The women of the house were busily employed in making cloth, and the men in preparation for a visit to Ulitea. Nothing was now in their mouths but the Arreoys, and the expedition to Ulitea. It was now considerably after midday, and as the people complained so much of their fatigue, it was agreed to stay there till the following morning. I endeavoured to amuse myself in the best possible manner, by walking about the neighbourhood : and at night, was accommodated in the best manner the hut afforded; that is to say, upon the sod or cold ground.

At sun-rise on the following morning, we again proceeded on our journey. Here again occurred the same obstacle which had impeded our progress on the former day : we had again to drag the boat over the coral rocks, the edges of which were as sharp as flints. By noon, with bloody feet and exhausted spirits, we reached the habitation of the chief of the island : this house was about one hundred and forty feet long, and fifty wide, being by far the largest on the island. The chief *kindly and hospitably received us ;* he ordered a small hog, and bread-fruit, to be immediately roasted, an order which our sailors evidently took in good part.

The chief, who is brother of Edeah, shewed me every possible civility, escorting me in his neighbourhood, and exhibiting his magazines. The sum total of his stores was five muskets, two pistols, three or four quart bottles of gun-powder, three or four pounds of gun-powder folded up in some country cloth, ten gun-flints, a hammer, pincers, and a few nails of different sizes.

We did not, however, get on with the main object of our voyage, the procuring hogs. There was but one kind of property which would procure them, and we were almost as scarce in this article as themselves. Muskets and gun-powder were the only currency. We spent the afternoon very agreeably with our host; and as the sailors found partners to their inclinations amongst the natives, they seemed in some degree more reconciled to their former fatigues.

On the following morning at sun-rise, after a suitable return, we again proceeded on our journey, accompanied by a native, whom we had taken with us at the request of Pomarrie. This man assured us that our sufferings were now at end, that we were within a very inconsiderable distance of his residence, where we should procure every thing the island produced, and as many hogs as we wanted. This intelligence was very seasonable consolation to us; every one exerted his utmost efforts to gain this Land of Promise. We at length arrived. It was a village by far the most considerable of any we had yet seen. The men and women were all and equally assiduous in rendering us their assistance. The boat was by this time scarcely able to hold water, so much was it injured by dragging it over the sharp rocks; the first business therefore was to haul her to land, and repair her, as far as our circumstances would admit. As this could not be finished till late in the evening, and the people received us with such an hearty welcome, our hog and bread-fruit being roasted on the spot, I resolved to remain there during the night, and recommence our journey on the following morning.

It has been before mentioned that not the least of our smaller kind of difficulties arose from the impertinent curiosity of the natives. It was necessary to show them every thing; and as they do not want cunning whenever the occasion demands it, they had no difficulty in inventing a plausible reason: unless they saw our articles of trade, they could not decide whether they were such as would suit them; and their hogs being in the mountains at a considerable distance, how could we expect them to bring them down at such an uncertainty?

Pomarrie's friend moreover informed them that I was very rich; they therefore insisted upon seeing every thing, and it was necessary to gratify them.

They were charmed at the sight of such wealth, and promised me that every thing should be ready for us on the following morning.

CHAP. XXVII.

Continuation of Occurrences at Eimeo.

I WENT to sleep with the treasure-chest close to my side, as usual. How great was my surprise when, awaking about two o' clock in the morning, I saw a fellow of unusual stature, walking off with it most deliberately! The fellow must doubtless have touched me, for I happened to awake in the moment that he was leisurely decamping with his booty. I immediately alarmed the house, and called my boat's crew; but as two of them had slept out, and two only were in the house, I knew not how to proceed. So enraged was I at this atrocity, that, seizing a piece of wood at hand, I followed the thief, and came up with him as he was in the act

of setting it down in a house full of
natives. Without any thought of consequences, I repaid him on the spot with
some heavy blows on the back; the natives started up and rescued him, and
wresting the stick from me, repaid
me in my own coin; my two fellows
standing petrified with terror. Having
no other resource but flight, I betook
myself in good earnest to my heels, and
gaining the house of the chief requested
him to interpose. From his reluctancy
of manner, I could entertain no doubt
that he had been accessary to the theft.
I in vain solicited him to accompany me
to the spot, and effect the recovery of
my chest.

Finding that entreaty had no effect,
I had recourse to other means, and seizing the boat's iron tiller, threatened that
I would put a period to the fellow's existence or lose my own, unless my chest

was restored. He now consented to
follow me. The whole village was by
this time in an uproar; the fellow himself, the original cause of the tumult, sat
triumphantly on the chest, and seemed
to glory in the heroism of his theft.

A most fortunate circumstance was,
that the fellow in taking the trunk,
had, at the same time, carried off the
two pistols with which I usually travelled,
and all the ammunition. It is not at all
improbable, that I should otherwise have
given him the contents, whilst in the
first transports of passion; a circumstance which must have been attended
with the most serious consequences, as
a general affray must then inevitably
have ensued. Indeed it was already
very near it, for the two men remaining with me, having resumed their courage, were now brandishing their knives
and vowing vengeance, till some of

the natives spoke of chastising them, and daring them to the issue. Finding that they were determined to stand their ground, I ordered my men to desist from provoking them; this had the happiest effect, for their anger subsided sensibly. I now laid great stress on my interest with my friends Pomarrie and Edeah, explaining their certain indignation, when they learned that I had been thus treated, in any part of their dominions. I informed them, that it was chiefly on their business that I was induced to visit the islands; this was in some measure true, being commissioned to bring them as much ava as possible. Never were the lives of any adventurers more in the power of savages, than were ours at this time, for our boat being hauled up a considerable way, it was almost as impossible for us to launch her, as to move the island.

I now clearly saw that it was a concerted scheme, and having no friends, I thought it best to desist from any violent measures. I again addressed myself to the thief, and this being ineffectual, again requested the interference of the chief; after being thus driven from one to the other, the fellow at length proposed to return it upon condition of receiving a recompence. I was compelled to capitulate; this circumstance concurred with others to convince me, that from the greatest to the least, the island was little more than a receptacle for thieves.

I could not but impute the whole of this scheme to the fellow whom I had taken with me at the request of Pomarrie, who had so artfully drawn us into this ambush. Disguising my suspicions, I offered him a passage back again, lest he should excite them to new outrages, and thinking that others were not as cunning as himself, he was persuaded to embark. After carrying him about a mile and an half, we resolved that he should swim for his perfidy, and we accordingly compelled him to take to the water; the fellow in the mean while protesting his innocence, and evidently apprehensive that he was about to be put to death.

We made a strong effort to reach Otaheite, but the wind being against us, and a very heavy sea, we were in danger of being swamped, and were therefore compelled to put back again. We took shelter in a cove nearly on the weather part of the island, and took up our lodgings in an old canoe. The people here treated us with great civility, though their means of supply was very scanty There appeared indeed a very general scarcity over the whole island.

From the first of our arrival, the weather had been very tempestuous, but
for the two last days it blew an hurricane, accompanied at times with rain,
thunder, and lightning.   Our lives were
doubtless preserved by our returning as
we did, for two of Pomarrie's canoes
were swamped by persisting in their attempts to make the passage, and every
man on board perished.

For powder or muskets I could have
had any quantity of hogs I wanted,
but they would trade for no other articles.

The weather at length becoming more
settled, we returned to Otaheite, after
an absence of nine days.

CHAP. XXVIII.

Observations on Eimeo.—Inferior much to Otaheite.—Preparations for an Expedition to Attaboura.

IN the mean time the captain and our shipmates had been very apprehensive for our safety. We complained heavily to Pomarrie and Edeah, of the perfidy of these islanders; they affected to lament this breach of hospitality, but it was all simulation. They recommended fire and devastation, the common mode of retaliation amongst those islanders. This mode of warfare, however, I thought most prudent to decline.

In this circuit around the island of Eimeo, I observed, that these islanders had but little to distinguish them from the Otaheitans. Tallow harbour is situated on the north-west side, and from a reef which surrounds it, in common with all the Society Islands, is somewhat difficult of access.

The entrance is most easy when the trade-wind blows fresh. Here and there may be found an opening sufficient to admit a ship, and this happens to be the case opposite Tallow harbour; there is here a sufficient opening and ample water for a first rate man of war. Once in the inside, there is no further danger to be apprehended, being perfectly landlocked, with space enough for half the royal navy of Great Britain.

It is impossible, however, to keep too good a look-out against the thievish propensity of the natives. In a word, the island is, in every respect, far inferior to Otaheite; it has not the same fertility, and nothing of the same hospitality in the reception of strangers.

I do not deny but that one cause of this latter defect might possibly be the comparative scarcity in the island of Eimeo; it was only here and there, that we could observe the bread and cocoanut tree, and at this time they seemed chiefly to exist on the mountain plantain and fish. Several of them were suffering very severely from dysenteries; perhaps this might be imputed to their diet. Wherever we stopt, we found that the main article of their subsistence was derived from the mountains and the sea.

Generally speaking, the hogs of Eimeo are larger than those of Otaheite: their tusks are immense, a circumstance which, added to their fierceness, renders them dangerous to approach. The island is governed by one of the relations of Edeah.   The Eimean women are, to all appearance, much more industrious than the Otaheitan females; many of them were employed in making cloth, and whole families in preparing for an approaching visit to Ulitea. It appeared to me to be but thinly inhabited, and for the same reason as Otaheite, the prevalence of infant murder.

In the very first discovery of this island, they exercised their thievish propensity on one of the goats of captain Cook; and as it was the invariable practice of this excellent man, as little to suffer as to do an injury, he demanded the thief and the stolen property from the receiver of the stolen goods, that is to say, of the principal chief of the island. The usual excuses of absolute ignorance were pleaded, and while the negociation was pending, a second goat was still more impudently stolen.   Exasperated

at this audacity, the captain threatened
the chief, that unless the stolen property
was immediately restored, and the thief
given up to his merited indignation, he
would destroy all the canoes on the
island: and this menace he was compelled to execute in part before he could
recover his goats.

It seemed natural to conclude, that
this example would have worked some
beneficial effect on their national character, and that future navigators would
not have been exposed to similar depredations; but unfortunately the roguery
of this people is beyond the healing
power of salutary correction, and they
will continue thieves as long as they shall
continue savages.

It was at this time that a circumstance
of a political nature occurred, which was
of good effect to us, as tending to confirm our men in their present quietness.

Pomarrie, and the people of Attahoura, as has been before mentioned, had made a peace in the year 1802. Pomarrie, however, had never wholly laid aside his designs of conquering them, and he had consented to the peace more from present convenience, and the advantage of procuring time to collect new resources, than from weariness of war, or from any pacific inclinations. The peace, therefore, was no sooner concluded, than he applied himself vigorously to collect the means of a new war, and by the time that our people had landed from the wreck, he had become almost prepared to enter upon action.

One thing alone remained to be done. What could he not effect when seconded by such allies as our sailors? He resolved therefore to spare no efforts to gain them. He explained his plans and the justice of his war, but justly concluding that they cared as little about the one as the other, he added the more powerful promise that the plunder should be theirs, hogs, women, and cloth. Our fellows could not withstand these temptations, and therefore agreed to follow him, and if necessary to fight for him. He next applied himself to the captain and me, and earnestly requested that we would lend him our assistance in so just and necessary a war.

As their private quarrels in no manner concerned us, we excused ourselves from his invitation, alleging that we had property to protect at Matavia. We informed him, however, that he was welcome to our boat and its materials, and as he saw that he could prevail on us no further, he thankfully accepted our offer. We added, however, that if his enemy should attack him either at Matavia, or Oparrie, his patrimonial estate, we would then defend him to the last extremity.

Satisfied with these assurances, in the beginning of August, 1803, Otoo, the king, his brother Tereinavouroa king of Tiarabo, Pomarrie, Edeah and her warriors, Paitia, the brother of Pomarrie, and Awow, his sister, together with ten Europeans, and all their adherents and fighting men, departed on this mighty expedition, leaving behind them some old women and fishermen to forage for the army. It was believed that, in the previous solemnities, no less than ten or twelve human sacrifices would be offered up to their gods upon this occasion. They proceeded forward in the most slow and cautious manner, measuring as it were every footstep.

It has been before mentioned, that their great idol Oro was kept in the moria of Attahoura, and being the great object of Otaheitan veneration, it is the general resort on all public solemnities. It is here that all their greater meetings are held, and their kings crowned; on which occasions human saccrifies are offered. The coronation of Otoo could not be complete till it was celebrated here; and the Attahourians, considering him as an usurper, had hitherto delayed it.

Terinavouroa, king of Tiarabo, died upon the march, leaving his wealth and government to his counsellor: his wife was very scantily provided, but being the cousin of Otoo, and the sister of the queen, she still continued to reside in the family. The greater part of his subjects, according to the custom of the country, came to the tupaow, or sepulchre at Oparrie, to pay their last respects to his obsequies. This tupaow is simply a stage supported on six posts, about four feet from the ground, the corpse being placed thereon in a sitting posture, arrayed in a scarlet dress, and during a certain period attended by his former servants. The surgeon of the missionaries had been this chief's adopted Tayo, and had there not been one law for strangers, and another for themselves, he ought, as such, to have succeeded to the greater part of the property of the deceased. On the other hand, he was wholly neglected; perhaps, as his talents were not those of a warrior, they considered him not a very suitable chief.

Many of the natives, as ridiculously as impiously, imputed his death to the prayers of the missionaries; for they are persuaded that many of them are thus killed. Edeah was much afflicted with his death, he having been her favourite, as Otoo was that of Pomarrie.

The royal army having now arrived in the enemy's country, the rebels, as they were pleased to term them, affecting ignorance of their intention, gravely demanded the purpose of their visit; to which they as gravely replied in professions of friendship. The Attahourans, however, were on their guard.

It is not easy to conjecture what would have been the event, had either party ventured a battle. But the party of Pomarrie had now so increased in numbers, that the Attahourans were daunted at their very sight. Part of them accordingly submitted; and, as by this desertion the remainder became too weak to venture any further contest, they were compelled to follow their example. The whole country was thus subdued: Pomarrie immediately dispossessed the principal chiefs of their lands, and divided them among his own friends. Edeah had a great part of these forfeited domains; and Innamo-tooa, the widow of Oripiah, the brother of Pomarrie, experienced in the same manner the royal munificence. She deserved it so well, that all but the sufferers joined in the praise of this act.

CHAP. XXIX.

Arrival of a Ship.—Death of Pomarrie.—
Character.

AFTER the unfortunate circumstance of the loss of our ship, our prospects at Otaheite were very gloomy. Having saved little or no property from the wreck, it became a subject of serious consideration in what manner we should subsist. Otaheite is as little calculated as Europe for those who are without money. It was moreover uncertain how long we should be compelled to remain in our present situation. To attempt building exceeded our means ; we had lost our carpenter at the Sandwich Islands, and it was in vain to expect any

assistance from any other of our people.
Our command and authority over them
had vanished since the wreck; every
one now followed his own way, and
appeared so attached to their present in-
dolent life, that they seemed to have no
intention of quitting it. Of the whole
of our former crew, the cook and mate,
the captain, and myself, were alone united
in a common cause, that of returning
to our native country. Our blacksmith
had set up for himself amongst the natives, and was in a very fair way of making a livelihood even in the worst of
times. It was unfortunately not so with
us; we knew it, but could not help
ourselves.

The blessing of Providence, however,
again interposed at a time that we had
almost ceased to hope; for after we had
been about three months in this suspense
of hope and fear, one afternoon a shout

of Te pahia, te pahia, A ship, a ship, re-
sounding through the island, aroused us
into new hopes. Hope and fear now alternately prevailed: our fears suggested
that the captain might have some possible objection; that he was going to China,
or some other more circuitous voyage.
It so happened, however, that the goodness of Providence was not incomplete;
the ship was going to the very place to
which of all others we wished to go, to
Port Jackson. We agreed with him for
a passage; and in our present situation,
laying aside all indignation at the conduct of our shipmates, we divided with
them our remaining property.

There had been so many ceremonies
to get through at Attahoura, that the
business had not been finally settled upon the ship's arrival. The intelligence
of this event, however, brought Pomarrie to Oparie to prepare his presents;

he had got his hogs in the canoe, and was half-way to the ship, when he was seized suddenly with a fit, and falling with each hand on the side of the canoe, expired. The poor fellows in the canoe immediately paddled back as fast as possible to his house at Oparie, where, in her way likewise to the ship, Edeah had by this time arrived. Messenger after messenger was dispatched to the missionaries and their surgeon; they were earnestly intreated to hasten to the house of Pomarrie. The surgeon happened at this time to be on board the ship, taking a farewell leave of us upon our departure. We earnestly advised him, should he find Pomarrie still alive, not to venture to prescribe to him; as in the case of his death the natives would not fail to impute it to poison, and perhaps avenge his supposed murder on the mission. It has been before mentioned, that they imputed the death of Terinavoura to the prayers of the missionaries; and that they are persuaded that the prayers of these holy men have this kind of sacred witchcraft. Under such impressions, it may readily be conceived that the situation of the missionaries is not the most enviable in the world.

Not one moment was lost on the part of the surgeon, who on his arrival found the whole of the family in the deepest anguish and distress. The brother of Pomarrie was deaf to all consolation, and could scarcely be withheld from suicide. All was anguish and confusion; some imputed his death to one cause, others to another; but the opinion of the majority was, that he had offended the Gods, though they could not agree by what means, except by his human sacrifices. They had recourse to one most singular remedy; the body of

an human victim which he had sacri-
ficed about three weeks before, was
brought and stretched prostrate under
him, in the hopes of appeasing the offended divinity.

The sudden and instantaneous death
of this man was not very unreasonably
imputed by some to the enormity of his
crimes, as well in this, as in other instances. Should these impressions continue,
the most beneficial effects may be expected. None had more cause of regret in
this event than the missionaries, to
whom Pomarrie had ever continued a
fast friend. They wrote to the captain
of the ship, requesting him to remain
till the morning, that the sense of the
society might be taken in what manner
to act upon this unexpected occurrence.
The captain thought that he should
lose nothing by compliance, and therefore consented.

The following morning Mr. Jefferson came to the ship, and informed us that after several consultations, the society had resolved to confide in the promises of Edeah, who said that every thing would doubtless proceed as before. Mr. Jefferson, at parting, requested me to desire their friends at home not to be over solicitous as to their safety. These were his words as far as I can remember them.

The Otaheitans will doubtless rack their brains to discover some probable cause of the death of Pomarrie; and, after other conjectures, will perhaps impute it to some magical power from the ship. Should any one amongst them make this assertion, I have no doubt that he would be immediately seconded by his brethren, so general is their belief of supernatural agency. On the decease of his son about a month before, they were firmly persuaded that he had been charmed to death by the missionaries. They are moreover convinced that the greater part of their plagues and diseases flow immediately from the shipping.

The loss of the missionaries in Pomarrie is I fear irreparable; but this is saying as much as can be said in his favour; for if he consented to a joint partnership with the missionaries, he fleeced his own subjects most unmercifully. Though this man possessed at least equal abilities with his father in things of a political nature, he was never able completely to subdue his enemies. They considered his government as an usurpation; and therefore never missed an opportunity of molesting his quiet. His affairs were thus not unfrequently in a very tottering situation.

The mutineers of the Bounty were a resource as fortunate as unexpected for the circumstances of Pomarrie. Being well skilled in the art of dissimulation, he had little difficulty in gaining them to his party, and with them an invincible advantage. His promises were unbounded; he had no scruple to promise, because he had no intention to perform. With the assistance of these *heroes*, for such were they considered by the natives, he was enabled to carry every thing before him; and in a very little time was acknowledged as king of the whole island.

Since this time there have doubtless been many risings and revolts; but upon the whole Pomarrie has prevailed over them all. Nor was this the only time that he was indebted for his safety to his European friends; as in the late war he would have been effectually ruined, had it not been for the assistance of the English, who happened at that time to be on the island. The enemy hitherto victorious through their assistance, were now compelled to sue for peace, and the affairs of Pomarrie again re-established.

With regard to his personal qualities, he was a savage of unusual address, and indeed grace and majesty. He had something of the appearance of an uncommon man; his general manners were very engaging, but under the appearance of candour he had too much of the hypocrite.

In his prosperity he was insufferably proud towards his enemies; and as a necessary effect of the same sanguine temperament of mind, was equally dejected in his adversity. A proof of this has already been mentioned in his determination to abandon the island upon a partial defeat. Nor was this the only instance, as under similar circumstances he frequently applied to captains to convey him from the island.

The most singular trait in his character, as a savage, was a species of prudence and foresight ; a mind which was capable of forming and adhering to a certain proposed rule of conduct. His conduct to the Europeans, and countenance of the missionaries, were the effects of this political genius. Resisting the first impulse, which would have tempted a savage to plunder them without formality and delay, he formed a more refined plan, that of encouraging and going shares in their present and future stock. This as effectually answered their purpose as his.

END OF THE SECOND VOLUME.

T. GILLET, Printer, Salisbury Square